DAYTRIP MISSOURI

A Travel Guide to the Show Me State

Written by
Lee N. Godley

Updated by
Patricia O'Rourke

Layout Design by
Patricia O'Rourke

Cover Design by
Brenda Bennett

Maps Created by
Paul Wentzel and Pat O'Rourke

Illustrations by
Debora Humphrey

Missouri Department of Natural Resources
Credit for listing of State Parks

DAYTRIP MISSOURI
SECOND EDITION

Aphelion Publications, Incorporated
5 Herring Drive
Fulton, MO 65251
(573) 642-4437
FAX (573) 642-6341

ISBN # 0-9651340-2-4

Introduction

*"**Daytrip Missouri**" has its roots in the vision of a young man, Lee Godley, Two months after the release of the first edition Lee died unexpectanly of an aneursym with his dream barely underway. The second edition of the book includes FAX numbers, Web Site numbers, as well as complete update information from each Visitor Bureau/Chamber of Commerce Director. The following paragraphs remain as Lee originally intended for the book series.   —PEO*

"Any traveler knows the value of pertinent, and exact information. And a good researcher can certainly appreciate a source that facilitates finding this information. *DM* was conceived as a traveler's tool. The authors' design was to condense mounds of brochures and pamphlets into an easy to read, easy to access publication that could be read, and tossed into the front seat of your car when you headed out to spend a day visiting one of Missouri's many "daytrip" opportunities. Unlike previous efforts, we chose to divide the state up into travel routes vice the more familiar regions. Thus, you will be able to reference by alphabetical order those sites along one of the major thoroughfares in the state. You'll find such helpful information as historical background, popular attractions, nearby attractions, special tour opportunities, and annual event listings.

The one item that sets *DM* into a class by itself is the insider tips from many of the Visitor Centers and Chamber of Commerce Directors around the state. These testimonies offer you, the prospective visitor, a personal insight and invitation to share in the adventure opportunities of that particular location. The idea was to offer you, the reader of *DM*, the kind of information that you can't find in a brochure.

Finally, *Daytrip Missouri* is intended to be a testimony to the dedicated workers — both volunteers and professionals — of this state who were involved in Missouri tourism. In truth, these dedicated individuals ARE the book you have just purchased. It was their avid involvement and participation that truly made *Daytrip Missouri* possible. For this, the authors, and now you the readers, will be forever grateful.

May this publication assist you as you enjoy the history, the culture, and the recreation opportunities that the ShowMe State offers. One does not need to travel to the far corners of the globe to experience the beauty of God's creation, the ingenuity of mankind, nor the excitement of the twenty-first century. Let *Daytrip Missouri* be your guide to visiting the great state of Missouri."

—Lee N. Godley

iii

Dedicated to Lee Godley
1952-1996

To Lee Godley and his daughters Angela and Chrissy.

Acknowledgments

I wish to express my appreciation to the many people who took part in the updating of this book. To Karan Godley who entrusted me to the task of updating the Missouri book. To each Visitor Center/Tourism Director, Chamber of Commerce Directors for submitting updated information, pictures, maps, asssiting in editing and proofreading materials. To Jeff Wohlt from the Missouri Division of Tourism who encouraged me. To the Department of Natural Resources for the permission to list all state parks and the year of their acquisition. To Debora Humphrey for her wonderful illustrations. Especially to my husband, Earl, who again allowed me the time to pursue the update and for his many hours of proofreading. Lastly, to all those who buy the book and have the opportunity to travel the great state of Missouri to see how blessed we "are to be Missourians."

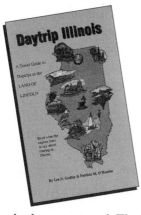

Daytrip Illinois

"Daytrip Illinois" by Lee Godley and Patricia O'Rourke is the second in a series of daytrip books published by the Aphelion Publishing Company. The Land of Lincoln, is a state that is literally a historic mecca. Whether you go to Springfield to witness the roots of Abraham Lincoln, or travel to Nauvoo to see firsthand the plights of the Mormons, or experience the hometown of Superman in Metropolis — Illinois offers something for everyone who loves to travel. The book is a must for any Chamber of Commerce, for any Visitor Center, for any public or school library and for any daytripper. *"Daytrip Illinois"* may be purchased from major bookstores, specialty shops or the Aphelion Publishing Company, Incorporated (573) 642-4437 or FAX (573) 642-6341.

Tourism Fuels Missouri's Economy

Drawn by Missouri's amazing diversity, travelers enjoy themselves at the state's lakes, historic sites, cities, and parks in growing numbers each year. And their pleasure is Missouri's profit, for tourism remains one of the state's top three revenue-producing industries — a major generator of spending, jobs, and tax revenue.

Travelers spend about 11 billion per year in Missouri, according to Division of Tourism data. All that spending means jobs for Missourians — nearly 300,000 jobs due to tourism, both directly and indirectly. The industry generated nearly $3.9 billion in state tax revenue in 1996 (the most recent year for which totals are available).

What does that mean to Missourians? Aside from jobs and business activity, the tax revenue alone has a major impact. It helps fund education, road repairs, health care, and other vital state services. If traveler spending stopped, the tax burden on Missourians would increase, simply to maintain essential state services.

Missourians, made up 31 percent of all Missouri travelers during 1996. The remaining travelers come mainly from surrounding states, crossing into Missouri to enjoy a short getaway trip (or a long vacation).

What brings them to Missouri? And brings them back again and again? In a short word, it's diversity. Or variety. Call it what you will — Missouri has it.

Some people think of sparkling lakes, crystal clear rivers and streams, rugged hills and fertile farmland. Others might picture big cities, pro sports, world-class shopping, and nightlife. And some look to Missouri for reminders of Mark Twain, Harry Truman, and Jesse James.

They're all right, but they're not seeing the whole picture. Missouri's diversity ensures that travelers can find virtually anything they want.

St. Louis and Kansas City offer all the big-city fun, coupled with small-town friendliness. They feature symphonies and theater, professional sports teams, museums, shopping that rivals with coast, and excellent cuisine, among their many attractions.

St. Louis' appeal includes riverboat restaurants, Laclede's Landing, and Forest Park (with its zoo, science center, art, and history museums). Kansas City is famed for its many fountains, Nelson-Atkins Museum of Art, Country Club Plaza, jazz, and barbecue.

With their urban excitement, the two metro areas are typical of Missouri's other cities, such as Springfield, Independence, St. Joseph, Columbia, Cape Girardeau, and Jefferson City.

But travelers who want to bypass city life find it's only a short drive to some of the country's most beautiful forests, lakes, and rivers. They're perfect for camping, hiking, hunting, and fishing.

For instance, there's plenty of water. Central Missouri's huge Lake of the Ozarks is one of the most popular lakes in America. With all its fun on or near the water, it's a start for water-lovers. There are large lakes throughout the state, fed by free-flowing rivers that are great for canoeing and floating.

Some of the brightest lights and excitement are out in the country, too. Millions of travelers each year head to Branson, America's new live music capital with over 30 theaters featuring nationally-known performers. Silver Dollar City, one of Missouri's three major "themed" fun parks, is at Branson as well. (The others are Kansas City's Worlds of Fun and Six Flags Over Mid-America near St. Louis.)

Missouri also is rich in history, best symbolized perhaps by the Gateway Arch in St. Louis. Missouri served as the springboard for America's westward expansion. Today's travelers can visit the Pony Express Stables in St. Joseph . . . Missouri's oldest, Ste. Genevieve . . . numerous Civil War battle sites . . . and Missouri's first capitol (in St. Charles) or current capitol (in Jefferson City).

Harry Truman's birthplace at Lamar and the Truman Library in Independence are among the reminders of famed Missourians. Mark Twain's boyhood home is in Hannibal. George Washington Carver is remembered with a national monument at Diamond. Daniel Boone's last home at Defiance still stands, as does Gen. John J. Pershing's home in Laclede and the Churchill Memorial in Fulton honors a famed non-Missourian who made history here with his "iron curtain" speech in 1946.

There's only one thing certain when listing Missouri's attractions: The list will never be complete. State parks, festivals, wineries, caves — they're all part of the big picture that is Missouri. They all contribute to the diversity that keeps travelers on the road in Missouri — and helps keep Missouri's economy in high gear.

—Lori Simms
Public Relations Manager
Missouri Division of Tourism
www.motourism.org

What Is A Daytrip?

By Nancy Lewis
Director Kingdom of Callaway Chamber of Commerce

Many people are opting to take a one day excursion several times a year rather than an extended vacation. One day excursions can be anything that interests you from antique cars to eagle watching along the river to shopping in picturesque villages.

Daytrips can be more fun than a well planned vacation because they give you a chance to explore your local area. When you explore you find great little restaurants, shops, history and local people with wonderful stories to tell. Communities that can't market themselves because of their size or close proximity to larger cities can be a wealth of rich history and often provide much better scenery than the interstates and major highways.

Some of these great communities have fairs and festivals, art and craft shows and other events that are great family entertainment and very reasonably priced. There are bed and breakfast inns in smaller communities that provide a quiet setting and a glimpse of yesterday's hospitality. The trails in our state parks and along old trails allow hikers and bikers the opportunity to view spectacular scenery and an opportunity to enjoy the natural wonders of the area.

Daytrips have become the mini-vacations of a hard working society regardless of income level. Extended vacations are very costly for the average household, and certainly difficult for most single persons. A daytrip for singles means that you can take a different friend along each time you go. There are no hassles with working into other people's schedules when only one or two days are involved. Budgets don't suffer major blows because lodging and meals are minimal and yet you get to enjoy a variety of things to do.

Families can work short trips into the family schedule much easier than extended vacations and certainly can add a mini-trip on short notice. Families can also take several daytrips and accommodate the tastes of each family member. For example, one trip can be to an amusement park for the children. The next trip might be an arts and craft show for Mom and the next an antique car show for Dad. Each trip makes the family member feel special and all other family members can certainly spend a day doing something that may not be their top priority.

Daytrips are positive for everyone. They provide communities, no matter what size or location, the opportunity to showcase their unique qualities and history. You will be amazed at the variety of things to do and the great people you will meet.

—*Nancy Lewis*
Director
Kingdom of Callaway
Chamber of Commerce

Harry S. Truman Home
Independence, Missouri

Contents
Daytrip Routes

Interstate 70

Interstate 44

Contents
Daytrip Routes

Missouri Facts

- State Bird: blue bird — chosen 1927.

- State Flower: hawthorn — chosen in 1923.

- State Fossil: crinoid — chosen in 1989.

- State Insect: honey bee — chosen in 1985.

- State Mineral: galena — chosen in 1967.

- State Motto: Salus populi suprema lex esto ("let the good of the people be the supreme law") — placed on state seal in 1822.

- State Musical Instrument: fiddle — chosen in 1987.

- State Rock: mozarkite — chosen in 1967.

- State Song: "Missouri Waltz" arranged by Frederick Logan, composed by John Valentine Floyd, words by J. R. Shannon, the song was chosen in 1949.

- State Tree: dogwood — chosen in 1955.

- State Tree Nut: black walnut — chosen in 1990.

Missouri Geography

- Missouri is the 19th state of the United States in total area: 69,674 square miles.
- The highest point in the state is at Taum Sauk Mountain: 1,772 feet above sea level.
- The lowest point in the state is near Arbyrd: 230 feet above sea level.

Satellite Locations

As you travel down the interstates you will find many interesting satellite attractions surrounding each featured community. They are listed below on the pages they occur. For additional information contact the Convention and Visitor Bureaus/Chamber of Commerce offices were they are located.

Interstate-70

Augusta 92
Belton 56
Blue Springs 57
Centralia 75
Clinton 113
Concordia 113
Defiance 93
Dutzow 92
Eureka 106
Excelsior Springs 57
Fleming Park 40
Glasgow 78
Grandview 57
Gray Summit 107
Higginsville 72
High Ridge 107
Hodge Park 57
Kearney 57
Keytesville 79
Kimmswick 107
Kingsville 57
Kirkwood 107
Liberty 57
Lone Jack 41, 59
New Franklin 11
Readsville 28
Richmond 72
Sibley 40
Smithville 59
St. Peters 93
Tipton 87
Warsaw 88

Wentzville 93
Weston 59
Westphalia 46
Williamsburg 28

Interstate-44

Ash Grove 150
Bolivar 150
Butler 139
Diamond 134
Doniphan 175
El Dorado Springs 139
Fort Leonard Wood 143
Leasburg 156
Mansfield 150
Neosho 133
Point Lookout 123
Potosi 156
Purina Farms 156
Republic 150
Sarcoxie 134
Stanton 157
Stockton 139
Straffort 150
Vienna 143
Waynesville 143

Interstate-55

Black Forest Villages 164
Bollinger Mill State
    Historic Site 163
Doniphan 174
Ellsinore 174

Hawn State Park 186
Jackson 164
Massey House 163
Mississippi County 178
New Madrid County 179
Perryville 165
River Ridge Winery 164
Rocky Holler 163
Scott County 179
Stoddard County 180
Trail of Tears State Park
    163
VanBuren 174

Interstate -29

Albany 192
Maysville 198
Plattsburg 199

Highway 36

Bethel 221
Canton 210
Carrollton 205
Florida 221
Jamesport 205
Kahoka 219
Laclede 206
Memphis 215
Novinger 215
Paris 221
Trenton 206

Missouri State Parks

The Missouri state parks system includes some of the strongest images of the state's people, places, and events. Missourians identify with their prominent sons, such as Thomas Hart Benton, and with the places that shaped the state's history, such as the first Missouri State Capitol; they recognize Missouri's outstanding beauty in Elephant Rocks, Ha Ha Tonka, and Onondaga Cave; and they remember spending time with their families at places such as Johnson's Shut-Ins or Pomme de Terre Lake.

These images distinctly identify Missouri and provide the central theme for what has been recognized as one of our nation's finest state park systems.

—Missouri Department of Natural Resources
Division of State Parks

The system welcomes you to call for more information on state parks and historic sites, call the Missouri Department of Natural Resources, toll free, at 1-800-334-6946. Below is a list of the state parks and the year they were added to the state park system:

1923 Arrow Rock State Historic Site
1924 Bennett Spring State Park
1924 Mark Twain State Park and Mark Twain Birthplace State Historic Site
1926 Montauk State Park
1926 Sam A. Baker State Park
1927 Meramec State Park
1928 Roaring River State Park
1932 Big Lake State Park
1932 Van Meter State Park
1932 Wallace State Park
1932 Washington State Park
1934 Lewis and Clark State Park
1937 Dr. Edmund A. Babler Memorial State Park
1937 Big Oak Tree State Park
1937 Pershing State Park
1938 Crowder State Park
1946 Cuivre River State Park

1946 Knob Noster State Park
1946 Lake of the Ozarks State Park
1952 Thousand Hills State Park
1952 Confederate Memorial State Historic Site
1952 General John J. Pershing Boyhood Home State Historic Site
1955 Hawn State Park
1955 Johnson's Shut-Ins State Park
1956 Lake Wappapello State Park
1957 Trail of Tears State Park
1957 Harry S. Truman Birthplace State Historic Site
1958 Battle of Lexington State Historic Site
1959 Table Rock State Park
1960 Pomme de Terre State Park
1960 Wakonda State Park
1960 Boone's Lick State Historic Site

1960 First Missouri State Capitol State Historic Site
1964 Graham Cave State Park
1964 St. Francois State Park
1964 Watkins Mill State Park and Watkins Woolen Mill State Historic Site
1965 Dunklin's Grave State Historic Site
1967 Elephant Rocks State Park
1967 Rock Bridge Memorial State Park
1967 Bollinger Mill State Historic Site
1967 Hunter-Dawson State Historic Site
1967 Towosahgy State Historic Site
1967 Union Covered Bridge State Historic Site
1968 Locust Creek Covered Bridge State Historic Site
1968 Sandy Creek Covered Bridge State Historic Site
1968 Fort Davidson State Historic Site
1969 Stockton State Park
1970 Felix Valle House State Historic Site
1970 Jewel Cemetery State Historic Site
1970 Sappington Cemetery State Historic Site
1973 Finger Lakes State Park
1974 Bothwell Lodge State Historic Site

1974 Castlewood State Park
1975 Battle of Athens State Historic Site
1976 Mastodon State Park
1976 Harry S. Truman State Park
1976 St. Joe State Park and Missouri Mines State Historic Site
1976 Jefferson Landing State Historic Site
1977 Dillard Mill State Historic Site
1977 Thomas Hart Benton Home and Studio State Historic Site
1978 Ha Ha Tonka State Park
1978 Deutschheim State Historic Site
1979 Robertsville State Park
1980 Prairie State Park
1980 Weston Bend State Park
1982 Onondaga Cave State Park
1983 Long Branch State Park
1983 Scott Joplin House State Historic Site
1984 Grand Gulf State Park
1984 Osage Village State Historic Site
1987 Katy Trail State Park
1990 Battle of Carthage State Historic Site
1991 Nathan Boone Homestead State Historic Site
1991 Taum Sauk Mountain State Park
1992 Big Sugar Creek State Park
1992 Illiniwek Village State Historic Site
1998 Route 66 State Park

Missouri State Map

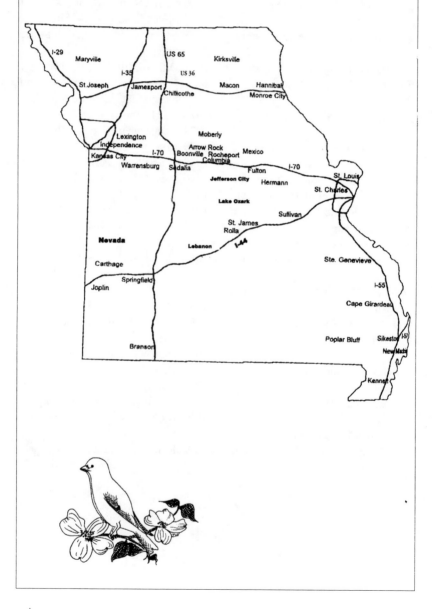

Daytrip Missouri
Interstate 70

Arrow Rock
"An Experience in Tranquility"

Location

Located on Highway 41 just north of Interstate 70 in Saline County.

History

Long before receiving its initial name of Philadelphia in 1829, the riverside locale served as a gathering place for Indians, and later settlers traveling along the Boone's Lick Trail. Later, the future town of Arrow Rock would serve as an outfitting point for those braving the westward expansion along the Sante Fe Trail.

Today, Arrow Rock is not just a place to visit; but an experience into the slow paced, peaceful lifestyle of yesteryear. Tranquility reigns supreme along its shaded avenues, where melodic song birds, and a host of friendly inhabitants all extend their unfettered hospitality to the watchful visitor. Clapboard walkways and well-kept paths offer the visitor convenient access to various antique shops, craft stores, museums, and refreshments. Guests, young and old alike, are seen mingling together in

The Restored J. Huston Tavern

Annual Spring Antique Market

harmony; each exhibiting that look of satisfaction in their discoveries.

➡ Getting Started

Begin your first visit to Arrow Rock at the Friends Information Center. It's on Main Street in the heart of town, right along the Boardwalk.

Attractions

J. Huston Tavern
(816) 837-3200
An 1834 restored Tavern offering food. Dinner reservations advised.

The Court House
This old log structure is shown by

guides in costume during the walking tours.

George Caleb Bingham House
The home of the renowned nineteenth-century, American artist was constructed in 1837 following his marriage.

Sappington's Museum
Hear the story of John Sappington, pioneer physician who popularized the use of quinine to treat fevers.

John P. Sites Home and Gunshop
See the home and shop of Johnny Sites, who, in 1844, moved to Arrow Rock and plied the trade of a gunsmith.

Friends Information Center
(816) 837-3231
Main Street
Artifacts and touring information are all available from this locale on Main Street.
✪ FREE ADMISSION

State Historic Site Interpretive Center
(816) 837-3330
A short walk from the heart of town, 19th century artifacts and educational dioramas await.
✪ FREE ADMISSION

The Lyceum Theatre
(816) 837-3311

This refurbished old Baptist church is now the site to witness the performance of Broadway-caliber plays throughout the summer months. It seats 400 people. Reservations required.

Special Tours

Five times a day during the summer months you can join an informative walking tour which takes in many of the attractions in Arrow Rock. Spring and fall months offer weekend tours. Tours begin at the Friends Information Center, and last an hour and a half. Group tours available by reservation. Call

A Broom Maker at the Fall Craft Festival

(816) 837-3231 for more information on these and additional tours of private restored homes.

Annual Events

May
• Antique Show—Antiques from all over the Midwest.

June-August
• Weekend Visiting Artists— Artists from throughout the Midwest demonstrate their talents and sell their wares along the boardwalk.
• Lyceum Theatre performances.

September
• Traditional Folk Music Festival and Workshops — Musicians from throughout the state exchange songs and instruments as they entertain.

October
• Heritage and Craft Festival — Artists from around the Midwest exhibit early American crafts.

December
• Christmas Hanging of the Greens
• Candlelight Tour of Oldtown

Shopping and Dining

Arrow Rock also offers an assortment of antique and craft shops along with a host of fine eating establishments. If your day trip runs out of daylight, there are an assortment of fine bed and breakfast facilities which you can retire for the evening. But make plans in advance. Camping is also available at the State Park.

In Conclusion

For more information contact:
Friends of Arrow Rock
PO Box 124
Arrow Rock, MO 65320
(816) 837-3231.
Web Site: www.arrowrock.org

Tips

✔ Parking is abundant at Arrow Rock but be careful of some of the stone gutters — for a car with a low front end, you can bottom out real easy.

✔ Many summer visitors like to get into town about 2 p.m., take in a leisurely stroll, catch a nice restful dinner, and then attend a play at the Lyceum.

✔ Make your reservations to eat or for the Lyceum in advance.

✔ The Emporium Ice Cream Parlor is a great place for the kids to play a game of checkers and enjoy a cone or two while the 'big folks' enjoy the adjacent antique shops.

Arrow Rock

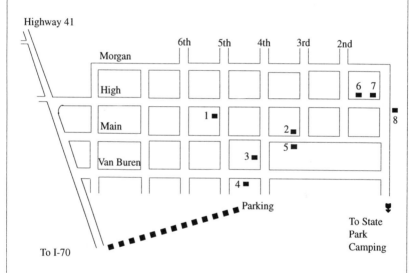

Highway 41

Morgan

6th   5th   4th   3rd   2nd

High

6 7

Main

1

8

2

Van Buren

5

3

4

Parking

To State
Park
Camping

To I-70

1. J.P. Sites Home and Gunshop
2. Friends Information Center
3. The Court House
4. State Historical Site Interpretive Center
5. J. Huston Tavern
6. Lyceum Theatre
7. Sappington Museum
8. George Caleb Bingham Home

66 I've lived in Arrow Rock thirteen years and I guess the comment I hear most often from visitors is how quiet and peaceful it is here. But what amazes me is that when Arrow Rock is as busy as Arrow Rock gets, say during theater time in the summer months, that's when people think it's quiet! As for me quiet comes in the Arrow Rock winter. Nothing can beat a walk by the spring valley with the snow flakes in the air, or being the first to walk by the spring after a snowfall. Currier & Ives has nothing on a snow-covered Arrow Rock! **99**

—*Kathy Borgman*
Executive Director
Friends of Arrow Rock

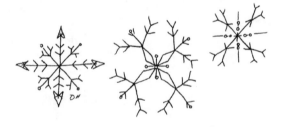

Boonville
"A Bridge to the Past"

Location
Along Interstate 70 and Exits 101, 103 and 106 North in Cooper County.

History
Long before the first American settlers arrived in 1810, tribesmen of the Osage and Missouri Indians roamed through the Boonville area. Those first American pioneers included the widow, Hannah Cole, and her nine children, who, along with her brother-in-law Stephen Cole and his family, constructed a fort on the shores of the Missouri River. A Spanish land grant enabled these pioneers to settle in an area later called the Boone's Lick Country — so named for Daniel Boone's sons who started a salt mining operation in 1806.

Boonville did not become a town until 1817. That year, Asa Morgan platted the town that was named to honor Daniel Boone. Note the later spelling of the town didn't include the 'e'. Reportedly, this stems from a local land deed signed by the famous frontiersman without the 'e'. The

Thespian Hall

actual State incorporation of Boonville however did not take place until 1839.

Remnants of Civil War history abound in Boonville. On June 17, 1861, Union General Nathaniel Lyon forced the surrender of the town from pro-Southern State Guardsmen.

Getting Started

Drop by the Boonville Chamber of Commerce located at 320 First Street. We will help you get started on your visit to Boonville by providing brochures, maps, etc.

Attractions

There are many sites to tour in Boonville, where more than 350 buildings are used with the National Historic Registry.

Ballantine House

High Street
Built in 1820's, it was a booming hotel in the hey day of the Santa Fe Trail.

Hain House.

Chestnut Street
The walnut log cabin was built in 1836 by Swiss immigrant, George Hain.

Harley Park

The park, established on land donated by William Harley in 1887, contains four Central Hopewell Indian burial mounds dating from 100 B.C. to 500 A.D. From adjacent Lookout Point you can see the Boonslick Salt Springs and the site of Old Franklin, which served as the eastern launching point for the Santa Fe Trail.

Kemper Military School and College

(816) 882-5623
701 Third Street
The roots of this outstanding military academy, oldest west of the Mississippi, go back to the 1840's.
✪ FREE TOURS

Old Cooper County Jail and Hanging Barn.

614 E. Morgan
Built in 1848, the old jail survived its function until 1978, when it was reportedly the oldest continuously used county jail in Missouri. Its most famous occupant was Jesse James, who called it home during a short stay in 1884.
✪ Open week-ends June through August. Memorial Day through Labor Day. Saturday 10a.m.-5p.m. and Sunday 1p.m.-4p.m.

Rosylyn Heights

(816) 882-5320
821 Main Street
This elegant 1875 mansion is the State Headquarters of the Daughters of the American Revolution. Tour reservations available upon request.

The Old Cooper County Jail

Open March 15 through 1st week in December. Sundays 1p.m.-4p.m.

Thespian Hall
(816) 882-7977
Main Street
The building originally housed an acting crew who gave their first performance on July 3, 1857. The massive building also served as both soldier quarters and hospital during the Civil War. Today, it functions as a center for community art programs, as well as the backdrop for the Missouri River Festival of the Arts.
☉Self-guided tours available.

Satellite Attractions

⚘ New Franklin
Laid out by Revolutionary War veteran, James Alcorn in 1828, it is located along Highway 40.

Rivercene
(800) 531-0862
County Road 463
An exquisite 1869 mansion built by riverboat Captain Kenny.

Special Tours

Cooper County Living History Tour
This self-guided driving tour takes you past more than 175 years of Central Missouri history. Route maps are available from the Boonville Chamber of Commerce.

Jites along the tour include:
- The McMahan Pioneer Cemetery of 1829 in Blackwater
- The Stagecoach Stop of 1860 in Billingsville
- The Dick's Mill of 1868 in Cotton Crestmead, an 1865 residence near New Lebanon
- Pleasant Green, an 1820 residence, which along with Burwood, an 1880 residence, are both located near Clifton City.
- Civil War Site in Otterville contains remnants of 1862 earthworks. Nearby a Jesse James train robbery took place.

Annual Events

April
- Big Muddy Folk Festival — National folk acts entertain at Thespian Hall.

June
- Heritage Days — Arts and crafts, along with an antique carnival, highlight a city-wide event.

July
- Cooper County Youth Fair — 4-H exhibits accompany this carnival.

August
- Festival of Arts — ballet, symphony and chamber music at Thespian Hall.

September
- Missouri River Valley Steam Engine Association Show — Antique tractors, crafts and a fiddling contest name a few of the events.

October
- Annual Festival of Leaves Arts & Crafts Show plus a Porkfest

December
- Annual Christmas Home Tours

Shopping and Dining

Boonville offers the antique and craft shopper an assortment of fine places to shop. Many are located in the downtown area — along Morgan, Spring, and Main Streets. For eating, along with an assortment of normal fast-food fare, there are a sufficient number of local diners.

In Conclusion

For more information contact:
Boonville Chamber of Commerce,
320 First Street 65233
(660) 882-2721
FAX 660 882-5560
email: boonchamb@c-magic.com
and
The Cooper County Historical Society Rt 1, Bunceton, MO 65237
(816) 366-4482.

Tips

✔ Main street has ample parking but can get congested at certain times in the day.
✔ A drive along the bluffs of Water Street will take you by many of the older Victorian style homes. From the bluffs, you get a spectacular view of the Missouri River.

Boonville

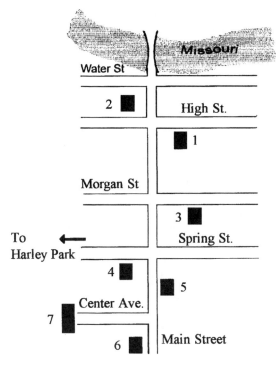

From I-70, Exit 103

1. Chamber Office
2. Ballentine House
3. Old Cooper Jail
4. Hain House
5. Thespian Hall
6. Rosyln Heights
7. Kemper Academy

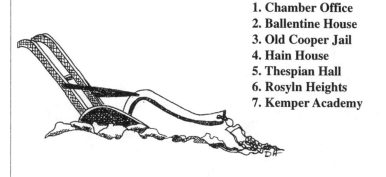

Columbia
"An Education in Culture and Fun"

Location

Located along Interstate 70 in Boone County.

History

Boone County's history is woven around the Boone's Lick Trail and later the Missouri Kansas and Texas Railroad. In 1815 settlers began pouring into the area in search of a quiet place to call home. The city was originally founded as the settlement of Smithton so named for General Thomas A. Smith. In 1821 a nearby town called Columbia was platted and eventually became the primary focal point of construction.

In 1835 the first school of higher learning, Columbia College, was established. But in 1837, Major James S. Rollins was influential in locating the first state university in Columbia. This began the outstanding tradition of the University of Missouri which assured Columbia's eventual growth.

Columns and Jesse Hall on Francis Quadrangale

➻ Getting Started

Begin your visit at the Columbia Convention & Visitor's Bureau at 300 South Providence. From Interstate 70, take the South Providence exit. The Bureau is located two blocks down from Broadway at the corner of Elm and Providence.

Attractions

Firestone Baars Chapel
Stephens College Campus
The chapel was designed by Eero Saarinen, who also designed the famous Gateway Arch in St. Louis.

Francis Quadrangle
(573) 882-6333
MU campus
Built in 1869, the Quadrangle is the site of the Chancellor's Residence, the Thomas Jefferson tombstone, as well as the Museum of Art and Archaeology and the Museum of Anthropology. The 18 surrounding buildings are listed on the National Registry of Historical Places.

Martin Luther King Jr. Memorial Gardens
(573) 874-7460
800 South Stadium Blvd
Located next to the MKT Trail, this garden contains walkways and an amphitheater with sculp-

tures that display Dr. King's writings.

Columbia Audubon Trailside Museum
(573) 875-1231
800 South Stadium Boulevard
Located near MKTrail and Martin Luther King, Jr., Memorial Gardens. Exhibits on birds, butterflies, rock samples, bird houses and other natural items and demonstrations.

Museum of Anthropology
(573) 882-3764
103 Swallow Hall on the MU campus
Artifacts of Native American culture along with Missouri history are displayed at this University attraction.

Museum of Art and Archaeology
(573) 882-3591
Pickard Hall MU campus
This popular exhibit contains an assortment of ancient and modern relics of art. More than 13,000 art objects representing all parts of the world and various periods of history are on exhibition.

Shelter Gardens
(573) 445-8441
1817 West Broadway
These gardens display more than 300 varieties of trees and shrubs and 15,000 annuals and perennials. During the summer months

United States Cellular Balloon Classic

the free Summer Garden Concert Series entertains each Sunday evening.

State Historical Society of Missouri
(573) 882-7083
1020 Lowery
Just the place to dig up your family roots. They have a vast library of census data and old Missouri newspapers on microfilm.
✪ FREE ADMISSION

Walters Boone County Historical Museum and Visitors Center
(573) 875-5268
Nifong and Ponderosa Streets

The museum houses a myriad of displays depicting frontier life in Boone county. A frontier spinning wheel and loom along with early portraits and photos relate the story of the county's early history. The museum also houses an assortment of antique toys, and an outstanding genealogical research library. Crafts people and musicians occasionally visit the museum to exhibit their talents.

Adjacent attractions include:

• **Montminy Gallery**
This gallery houses an assortment of paintings by Tracy and Pierre Montminy. You can also see historic photographs, negatives, and

paintings by local contemporary artists.

• **Maplewood**
Located just north of the museum is the Victorian home of Slater Ensor Lenoir and his wife, Margaret Ann Bradford. Mr. Lenoir came to Boone county from North Carolina in 1834. His house, built in 1877, has been restored to its original decor. Grounds feature original out-building, hay and horse barn, along with a petting zoo.

Attractions

Columbia Entertainment Company
(573) 474-3699
1800 Nelwood Drive
Local talent provides musical and drama throughout the year. They also have a school for dramatic arts for children and adults.

Maplewood Barn Theater
(573) 449-7517
Nifong Park
Outdoor drama for the entire family is performed during the summer. Be sure to bring blankets or lawn chairs for this theatre under the stars.

Missouri Symphony Society
(573) 875-0600
203 South Ninth Street

Quality musical performances feature renowned artists at the historical downtown Missouri Theater. June and July summer music festival every Friday evening plus the popular Pops Concert and Kids Concert.

Rhynsburger Theatre
(573) 882-7529
129 Fine Arts Building
Classical drama by visiting actors and students highlight the school years while summer months offer MU's Repertory Theatre.

Stephens College Playhouse and Warehouse Theater
(573) 876-7199
100 Willis
Professional and student productions of a variety of plays are staged throughout the year.

University Concert Series
(573) 882-3875
Jesse Hall MU campus
World class performing arts and events include everything from international ballet to musical ensembles.

Art Attractions
Columbia boasts a variety of outstanding art exhibits. The following galleries attest to this.

Bluestem Missouri Crafts
13 S. 9th Street
(573) 442-0211

Museum of Art and Archaelogy in Columbia

Columbia Art League Gallery
(573) 443-8838
1013 East Walnut

**Columbia College Art
Center Gallery**
(573) 875-7517
North 10th Street

Cool Stuff
(573) 875-7912
808 E. Broadway

Davis Art Gallery
(573) 876-7173
1220 East Broadway

Dauphine Gallery
(573) 443-8205
918 E. Broadway

Davis Art Gallery
(573) 876-7173
Walnut & Ripley Streets

George Caleb Bingham Gallery
(573) 882-3555
Fine Arts Building, Missouri
University Campus

Legacy Arts & BookWorks
(573) 442-0855
1010 E. Broadway

Missouri Art Gallery
(573) 443-5010
9 N. 10th Street

Montminy Gallery
(573) 443-8936
3801 Ponderosa Street

Museum of Anthropology
(573) 882-3764
100 Swallow Hall

Museum of Art & Archaeology
(573) 882-3591
Pickard Hall, UMC

Mythmaker Gallery
(573) 449-7870
216 South 5th Street

Poppy
(573) 442-3223
914 E. Broadway

Rogers Gallery
(573) 882-7224
Fine Arts Building, MR Campus

Studio of Gail Shen
(573) 442-9478
5 S. 9th Street

Walters-Boone County Historical Museum
(573) 443-8936
3801 Ponderosa Street

Natural Attractions

Another popular activity in the Columbia area is to visit one of its many parks. There is an excellent variety of hiking and biking trails in the parks for your family to enjoy.

Finger Lakes State Park
(573) 443-5315
Highway 63

The 1,100-acre recreational park is a mining reclamation project. Nearly a dozen small, isolated lakes have been joined together by a series of dams and canals. Hiking, biking, swimming and canoeing are all available, along with offroad riding areas for motorbikes and ATV's.

Rock Bridge Memorial State Park
(573) 449-7402
Highway 163
A quarry near the Little Bonne Femme Creek operated in the mid-1800's with an adjacent village consisting of a grist mill, blacksmith shop and general store. Today at the park you'll get a chance to see places like the Rock Bridge, the Devil's Icebox, and the Gans Creek Wild Area.

Three Creeks Conservation Area
(573) 882-9880
Highway 63 South on Deer Park Road
Camping, horseback riding, interpretive trails and even a cave await you on this 1,277 acre state forest.

Twin Lakes Recreation Area
(573) 445-8839
2500 Chapel Hill Road
Enjoy swimming, boating, fishing, walking and nature study on this 60-acre site.

Annual Events

January
- Columbia Entertainment Company Theater & MU Jesse Concert Series Opens
- Columbia Business EXPO
- Shakespeare's Gymnastics Festival
- Martin Luther King Celebration With Candlelight March

February
- Cat Classic Gymnastic Tournament
- MU & Stephens Theatres Open
- Ozark Anglers All Sport Show
- Home Builders Association Home and Garden Show
- Missouri Deer Classic

March
- Annual Spring Crafts Show — Mid-Missouri's largest spring craft show
- Taste of Mid-Missouri
- Showdown Sportsfest

April
- Earth Day

May
- Memorial Weekend — Salute to Veterans Parade & Airshow
- British Car Show

June
- Annual Art in the Park Fair — Central Missouri's largest outdoor fine arts fair, activities for all ages.
- Civil War Reenactment
- Twilight Festival — Music and other forms of entertainment each Thursday evening during June.

- Shelter Gardens Summer Concert Series Opens — Every Sunday evening in June and July.
- Boone County Fair & Horse Show — A chance to watch tractor pulls, fine horses, and live music.

July
- Fire in the Sky
- Show Me State Games — This popular event features athletes of all ages from around the state of Missouri competing in a myriad of events.

August
- United States Cellular Balloon Classic — Featuring morning and evening launches, after dark glow, food and entertainment, plus special shapes. The Balloon Classic benefits the Ronald McDonald House.

September
- Boone County Heritage Festival — Fun-filled activities are at Nifong Park.
- Columbia Festival of the Arts — Featuring children's area, dance and musical performances, fine arts and crafts demonstrations. Displays and sales of original fine art.

October
- Hartsburg Pumpkin Festival

November
- Fall Craft Show
- Kings Daughters Holiday Festival
- Sparkling Arts Holiday Show —Art gifts for all ages

December
- Downtown Holiday Festival
- Candlelight Tour of Maplewood
- Jubilee Arts for the Holidays
- First Night Columbia 1998

Shopping and Dining

Anchored by the Columbia Mall and charming vibrant downtown, you'll find more than enough places to shop and drop. From antiques to flea markets, from gourmet to fast food, shopping and eating facilities are adequately dispersed throughout the Columbia area.

The downtown area embraces 15 square blocks and offers the largest number of outdoor dining venues in Central Missouri. An authentic candy shop, designer cookie store and old fashioned pie bakery will satisfy any sweet tooth. As Columbia's cultural center you will find numerous galleries, an abundance of shopping and museums. It is truly a kaleidoscope of sights, sounds, tastes, and experiences for visitors of all ages.

In Conclusion

For further information contact:
Columbia Convention and
Visitors Bureau
300 South Providence
PO Box N- Dept DTM
Columbia, MO 65205
(573) 875-1231
FAX (573) 443-3986
1-800-652-0987
CVB@sockets.net

Tips

✔ Columbia is not a large metropolitan city. However, it is not exactly a small rural hamlet. Preplanning will enhance your accomplishments. Keep in mind that when the colleges and university are in session, there are more than 30,000 additional inhabitants to contend with. So, though the summer months are hotter, you may find them more attractive with less traffic.

✔ Most of the attractions are spread out, so plan your travel routes ahead of time. Parking is more than adequate at many facilities, and downtown has added a new parking structure. However University parking is a greater challenge, but the Columbia Visitors Bureau has MU maps that show visitor parking.

66 The things that make Columbia a great place to live also make it a terrific place to visit. A unique blend of rural hometown and urban sophistication, Columbia is pleasing to visitors of all generations. You will find an abundance of superb shopping in Columbia.

Our trails and parks are popular for hiking/biking. The city is known for its variety of fine dining, unique cafes and casual restaurants. Local night spots offer diverse venues for live music from contemporary to country. Leisure opportunities abound throughout the year with art and heritage festivals, concert series, theater productions, and historic sites.

Sports play an important role in Columbia. We are proud to host the Show-Me-State Games, collegiate sports, state high school athletic tournaments, equestrian competitions, shooting matches, and other contests year round.

There truly is something for everyone in Columbia. Visit us soon and you'll know why we say "Columbia for All the Things You Are!" **99**

—Renee Graham
Tour and Travel Manager
Columbia Convention & Visitors Bureau

A. Columbia College
B. Stephens College
C. University of Missouri Campus
   Museum of Art and Archaeology
   Museum of Anthropology
   Columns at Francis Quadrangle
D. Maplewood Home — Boone
   County Historical Museum
E. Martin Luther King Memorial
F. MU Faurot Field/Hearnes Center
G. Shelter Insurance Gardens
H. Columbia Mall
I. Historic Downtown
J. Columbia Regional Airport
K. Convention & Visitors Bureau
   Visitors Information Center

Columbia

Fulton
"A Kingdom in the Heartland"

Location

Located along Highway 54 just 7 miles south of Interstate 70 in Callaway County.

History

Callaway County was named for Captain James Callaway, who was killed in 1815 during an Indian attack at nearby Loutre Creek. Early in Callaway's history, the French had established a small community along the Missouri River at a place called Cote Sans Dessein. Callaway was officially formed in 1820 with the county seat established at Ham's Prairie. Later, the county seat was moved to a town called Volney, which was changed to Fulton in honor of the steam engine's principal inventor Robert Fulton.

The county became principally populated with settlers removed from Kentucky and Virginia. Therefore, when the Civil War broke, it was no surprise that sentiments were deeply pro-South. The Civil War gave birth to the legend of the Kingdom of Callaway. In 1862, Federal troops were confronted by several old men and boys armed with hunting weapons and a few "Quaker Guns." Records relate that a non-aggression treaty was negotiated and signed by both sides. Tradition has it that this independent treaty qualified Callaway as a free and sovereign kingdom.

History is everywhere in Callaway. Its winding roads will take you back in time to an era where the sun, not the hands of a clock, was the most watched thing in the course of a day. When you begin your exploration of Callaway you will begin to appreciate just how many miles traverse its boundaries.

➡️Getting Started

You can start by visiting the Callaway County Chamber of Commerce, which is located at 409 Court Street. We will provide maps or tour information to help you on your way.

William Woods University

Attractions

William Woods University
(314) 642-2251
200 West 12th Street

Drive through the scenic 170 acre campus of William Woods University, an independent, selective, coeducational institution founded in 1870. Water fowl enthusiasts will appreciate the various species of ducks, geese, and swans inhabiting Senior Lake.

The University's internationally known equestrian science program hosts national horse shows each year. Call for show schedules or an appointment to tour the equestrian science facilities and see the more than 100 horses of various breeds housed on campus.

Known also for its outstanding Fine Arts Department, the on-campus art gallery hosts numerous exhibitions throughout the year. Call the university for a copy of the

Winston Churchill Memorial

gallery schedule. 1-800-995-3159
Web Site: www.wmwoods.edu

Winston Churchill Memorial and Library
(573) 592-5369
Web Site: www.wcmo.edu
Westminster Campus
One of the primary points of interest in Fulton located on the campus of Westminster College. The Memorial is a rare opportunity to experience a bit of English history without crossing the Atlantic. The 17th century Church of St. Mary, the Virgin, Alderman-bury was designed by the noted British architect, Sir Christopher Wren. After surviving the blitz-krieg of WWII, the building was dismantled and reconstructed on the campus of Westminster College. It became a backdrop to Sir Winston Churchill's famous "Iron Curtain" speech, and later witness to noted speakers includ-ing many Presidents—Harry S. Truman, Gerald R. Ford, Ronald Reagan, and George Bush. Former Prime Minister of England Margaret Thatcher and Russian President Gorbachev have been among the noted speakers.

Another feature at the attraction is a 32 foot section of the Berlin Wall donated and sculpted by Edwina Sandys, granddaughter of the famous British statesman Sir Winston Churchill.

The Kingdom of Callaway Historical Society Museum
(573) 642-0570
513 Court Street, P.O. Box 6073
Newly opened March of 1998. The museum area depicts the history of Callaway County. There is a work area for genealogical research within the museum. Visitors are welcome.
✪ Call to inquire about hours

Missouri School for the Deaf Museum
(573) 592-4000
MSD campus
See the proud history of this state institution established in 1851.
✪ Tours available upon advance request.

Auto World Museum and Kingdom Expo Center
(573) 642-2080
P.O. Box 135
1920 N. Bluff Street
The museum is home to more than 90 rare cars including a 1931 Marmon, a 1895 Haynes, a Hudson pick-up, and fire trucks. The local collection and colorful exhibits include interesting characters who are part of the color of the Kingdom of Callaway. More than 4,000 visitors have found their way to the museum since it opened. Summer hours are Monday through Saturday 11:00 a.m.-5:00 p.m. Sunday 12:30 p.m.-4:00 p.m. Winter hours are Monday-Saturday 10:00 a.m.-4:00 pm;

Auto World Museum and Kingdom Expo Center

Sunday 12:30 p.m.-4:00 p.m.
✪ Groups welcome—there is an admission charge

Satellite Attractions

🌾 **Readsville**
Named in 1856 for postmaster John A. Read this town is located along Highway D.

Readsville Trading Post
Where you can experience that country store aura of yesteryear.

🌾 **Williamsburg**
Originally settled in 1828, this town is located east of Kingdom City along Interstate 70.

Cranes Store
This old turn-of-the-century store contains an antique toy collection, along with that old-time store atmosphere.

Special Tours

Callaway County Driving Tour
Old grave yards along with relic churches, school houses, surviving homesites and country stores all await the motorist in a tour of the county. Calwood is the site of the Civil War battle of Moore's Mill. A scenic drive along Highway 94 will take you past the 1831 settlement of Portland, which was a boom town in the early days of the steamboat. The Toledo Church was once a hide out for the outlaw Jesse James, who taught choir in the old church that still stands. The 1808 French settlement of Cote Sans Dessein was the initial site for the state capital until bigger money spoke in Jefferson City. Reform is the home for Missouri's only nuclear power plant.

Court Street Homes

Many of the gracious homes that line this street were designed by the state-wide noted architect, M. Fred Bell. Call the Chamber or Hollrah Enterprises to arrange for tours. (573) 642-8829

Natural Attractions

Biking along the many rural scenic roadways will reward the cyclist with many stunning views. Or if you would prefer the slower paced event, try hiking one of the many trails in Callaway County, imagining yourself as a member of the Lewis and Clarks expedition. Below are some of the natural attractions.

• Cedar Creek Hiking Trail
• Katy Trail State Park
• Mark Twain National Forest
• Whetstone Creek Wildlife Area

Annual Events

June
• Auxvasse Lions Club Rodeo — Three days of fun and excitement
• Auxvasse Truck and Tractor Pull
• Art Festival — Sponsored by the Fulton Art League
• Kingdom Days — Three day festival based on a Civil War confrontation between a Union General and the local militia. Humorous reenactments, crafts, entertainment, auto show, children's events and much more.

August
• Callaway County Fair

September
• Mokane Fair — Carnival rides and parade highlight the event.
• Fulton Jazz Festival — Jazz performers from around the state participate.

October
• Hatton Craft Festival — Crafts people from all over the Midwest attend this one day event.

December
• Fulton Christmas Parade

Shopping and Dining

In Fulton and throughout the county you will find an adequate assortment of delightful facilities to shop for antiques. Fulton is your best bet for lunch.

In Conclusion

For more information and updates about annual events contact:
Kingdom of Callaway
Chamber of Commerce
409 Court Street
Fulton, MO 65251
1-800-257-3554
(573) 642-3055
Web Site:
   http://www.ktis.net/~cocommer/
E-mail: commer@ktis.net
FAX: (573) 642-5182

✔ Parking is free and abundant around the sites to see.

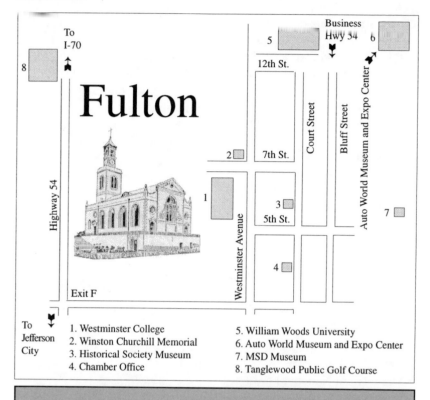

Fulton

To I-70

8

Highway 54

Exit F

To Jefferson City

2

1

Westminster Avenue

7th St.

3
5th St.

4

5

12th St.

Court Street

Bluff Street

Business Hwy 54   6

Auto World Museum and Expo Center

7

1. Westminster College
2. Winston Churchill Memorial
3. Historical Society Museum
4. Chamber Office

5. William Woods University
6. Auto World Museum and Expo Center
7. MSD Museum
8. Tanglewood Public Golf Course

66 Freedom and independence are themes that continually find their way into your subconcious as you travel Callaway County. From the secesssion from the Union during the Civil War to the Winston Churchill Memorial that dominates the Westminster College campus, the proud heritage of a free people combined with their warmth and humor will welcome you into our community and give you the feeling that you belong here.

Numerous events and festivals are spread throughout the year. All of these events center around families enjoying a variety of entertainment and interests.

Whatever your interests from golf, antique autos to shopping for antiques and unique gifts, Callaway County offers quality and warm friendly people that welcome you to the community and make you feel as though you're welcome. 99

—*Nancy Lewis, Director*
Kingdom of Callaway County Chamber of Commerce

Hermann
"A Taste of the Old Country"

Location
Located at the juncture of Routes 100 and 19 in Gasconade County.

History
Hermann was founded in 1836 by the German Settlement Society of Philadelphia. The group was made up of Philadelphian Germans and German-Americans who grew concerned over their children's proclivity towards Americanization. Exercising their new found freedoms in the land of democracy, the group sought out a site in the nation's interior on which to recreate and instill within their children the language and culture left behind in Germany.

Agents were sent as far away as Texas and Wisconsin to find a place to build their version of the Old Country. One agent, George Bayer,

The Herman Skyline

journeyed from St. Louis up the Missouri River that summer. The high bluffs along the river no doubt reminded a homesick Bayer of previous trips up the Rhine. When he ventured onto shore at the present site of Hermann, all he found was a small settlement of French trappers. However, caught his interest — grape vines growing up to 36 inches in diameter. The hilly location was deemed a perfect spot for the production of wine, and the town of Hermann was born.

Bayer proceeded to purchase 11,000 acres, at a dollar an acre, to entice the immigrants to settle this "Little Germany in America." In time, scores of German immigrants flocked to the little settlement in the Frene Valley. Though the effort for survival proved to be much more demanding than their previous homes back in Germany, the immigrants nevertheless persisted and eventually tamed the land in what would later become a part of Gasconade County.

➡Getting Started

We suggest that visitors begin their tour of Hermann from the Visitor Center located in the historic German School building situated on the corner of 4th and Schiller Streets in the heart of downtown Hermann. Brochures and maps are available as well as walking tour maps, lodging, restaurant, shopping and winery information. The Center is open daily from 9:00a.m. to 5:00p.m. The toll free number for Visitor Information is 1-800-932-8687.

Attractions

Deutschheim State Historic Site
(573) 486-2200
Tours beginning at the Museum shop will take you to some of the restored homes of early Hermann. The Pommer-Gentner House, built in 1840, is included on the tour. This well preserved home is reportedly one of the finest examples of German Neoclassical houses in the Midwest. Also on the tour is the Strehly House and Winery. Originally built from 1842 to 1869, the home and winery contain period decor as well as picturesque gardens. Adjacent gardens have grape vines planted in the 1850's still bearing fruit. A German speaking guide is available by prior arrangement.

German School Building
(573) 486-2017
Constructed in 1871, the building served as a school up until 1955. Various rooms within the school have been renovated to display an assortment of nineteenth century artifacts and artwork. The museum

Hermann "Wurstjaegers"

also houses a craft shop. The Visitor Center is now located in this building.

White House Hotel

(573) 486-3200

The 1868 hotel has been restored to its Victorian appearance and contains many of its original furnishings. A Victorian Ice Cream Parlor and Antique and Gift Shop are also contained in the multi-storied structure.

Show-Boat Theater

(573) 486-2744

At the theater, the cast of Show-Stopper Revue offers a lively, nostalgic musical, comedy presentation. This montage of music from the 40's - 60's is performed several times a month throughout the summer and early fall. You need to phone in advance for schedule and ticket information. (Groups of eight or more need to call (573) 486-5075)

Special Tours

Prior to prohibition, Hermann was reportedly the nation's second largest wine producing region. The making of wine was always important to these people who brought their wine-making skills from the old country. Their skillful legacy survives in the four wineries operating in Hermann today. All offer guided tours and fine restaurants.

Stone Hill Winery
(800) 909-9463
Established in 1847, Stone Hill at one time in the 19th century was the third largest winery in the world. Today it is the largest winery in the state of Missouri and third largest awarded winery in America.

Hermannhof Winery
(573) 486-5959
Located on the eastern edge of town, Hermannhof has been producing excellent wines since 1852. The century-old stone and brick building is still in operation.

Adam Puchta Winery
(573) 486-5596
The sixth generation of Puchtas have been operating this facility since 1855. Here you can still see an original stone-wheeled grape crusher and wine press.

Bias Winery
(573) 834-5475
A relative newcomer to the Hermann wine making tradition, the Bias winery was established in 1980, and today overlooks the Missouri River from the bluffs east of Berger, a satellite village.

Robller Winery
(573) 237-3986
Although located in the community of New Haven, 15 miles east of Hermann, the winery is part of the Hermann Vintners Association. The family owned winery is located in a quaint, country setting featuring a wonderful view of the rolling hills overlooking the vineyards.

Annual Events
There are literally scores of events occurring within Hermann during the course of a year, each garnished with a touch of Germany. The following are a list of the major events that occur annually.

May
• Maifest.— This well attended German celebration the third week of May includes German food, music, dancing, special activities for children, and craft displays.

June
• Annual Quilt Show — Quality quilts and their quilters gather on the fourth weekend of the month. Antique and new quilt display, contest and sale.

July
• Cajun Concert on the Hill — Three days of Cajun-styled music and dancing takes place at the Stone Hill Winery.

August
• Great Stone Hill Grape Stomp — Ever have the desire to feel grapes squishing between your toes? Try this annual event at the Stone Hill Winery.

October

• Oktoberfest — At the grand-daddy of all Hermann events, Four weekends in October you can experience a variety of music, food, and crafts in a festive atmosphere attended by thousands from all over.

December

• Kristkindl Markt — The first weekend of the month showcases a German Christmas market.

Shopping and Dining

For the avid shopper, you'll find Hermann full of antique, craft, and specialty shops throughout. Most of the stores are located in the downtown area. However, some excellent places are just a short drive away. Many of the touring attractions also contain gift shops. One would expect fine German cooking in a place like Hermann. Rest assured — your appetite for bratwurst will not go neglected in many facilities.

In Conclusion

For further information contact:
Hermann Visitors Center
PO Box 104
4th and Schiller Streets
Hermann, MO 65041
(573) 486-2772
(800) 932-8687
FAX (573) 486-5363

Tips

✔ Other than festival times, the traffic seems fairly light and parking is abundant and free.

✔ Hermann's designers drew up the town prior to actually seeing the area. The present layout confirms this. When you come to Hermann, you'll see a street that starts, and then runs right into a hill; only to start up on the other side again.

✔ Many of the major attractions are located within walking distance of the Visitor's Center.

✔ Save the winery tours for later in the day after exploring Hermann's history.

✔ Ocktober in Hermann is a very popular event, so be sure to get there early. With more than 50,000 visitors attending, traffic begins to back up early — especially for those needing to cross the river.

✔ Try this trip in the fall for a doubly rewarding experience. From the Stone Hill Winery you get a gorgeous view overlooking the town which is greatly enhanced with the fall foliage.

❝ Although famous for its festivals, Hermann offers visitors a wealth of things to see and do year round. Today, Hermann area vintners are again producing world-class wines.

Visitors can learn more about Missouri's German heritage by visiting the fascinating museums. Also, scores of beautifully restored historic homes, now bed and breakfasts, welcome guests. Bargain hunters and collectors will find antique and specialty shops to explore. **❞**

—Julaine Cabot
Tourism Director
Hermann Visitors Center

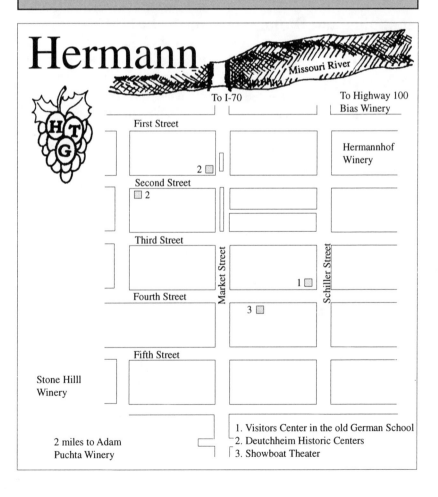

Hermann

Missouri River

To I-70

To Highway 100
Bias Winery

First Street

Hermannhof
Winery

2 ▫

Second Street

▫ 2

Third Street

Market Street

Schiller Street

1 ▫

Fourth Street

3 ▫

Fifth Street

Stone Hilll
Winery

2 miles to Adam
Puchta Winery

1. Visitors Center in the old German School
2. Deutchheim Historic Centers
3. Showboat Theater

Independence
"Where the Trails Start and the Buck Stops"

Location
Located east of Kansas City along Interstate 70.

History
Another of the larger cities that makes for an excellent daytrip is Independence. From its earliest designation as the "City of Zion" by Joseph Smith, through the tragedy of the Civil War and on into the more recent legacy as the home of Missouri's own Harry S. Truman, Independence has witnessed an avalanche of American history.

Independence became the county seat of government for Jackson County back in 1827.

By 1831, the city became a sacred haven for pioneers of the Church of Jesus Christ of Latter Day Saints. Though Smith's followers were forced out of Missouri in 1838, they returned after the Civil War and planted their legacy in the form of the Reformed Latter Day Saints Auditorium and Temple.

Independence saw two major battles during the Civil War. Both took place in the Square area. The Square also became a camp ground in 1863 when refugees, forced out of their homes by the enforcement of Order #11, pitched their tents around the area where the courthouse now stands.

Independence has seen its share of famous visitors. Famous guerrilla leader William Clarke Quantrill and Frank James were temporary residents of the local jail.

More recently, in Independence the career of one of this century's most popular figures — Harry S. Truman. His political involvement started in 1922 at the Jackson County Courthouse. The east side of the Courthouse continues to be a popular backdrop for politicians to eulogize the 33rd president.

➥ Getting Started
The hub of touring activity in Independence is located in the downtown area known as Historic Independence Square where you will find many historical attractions. Tickets and other information can be obtained at the Truman House Ticket Center located at the corner of Main Street and Truman Road.

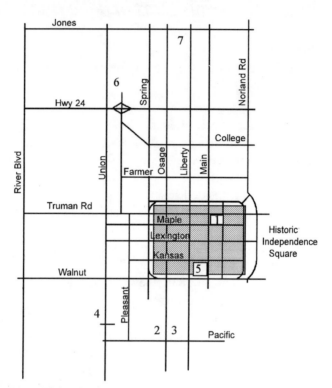

Independence

1. Truman House Ticket Center
...1859 Jail, Marshall's Home and Museum
2. Bingham-Waggoner Estate
3. National Frontier Trails Center
4. Church of Jesus Christ of Latter Day Saints
5. 1827 Log Courthouse
6. Truman Library and Museum
7. Vaile Mansion

Attractions

Bingham-Waggoner Estate
(816) 461-3491
313 West Pacific
From 1864 to 1870, the famous early-American artist, George Caleb Bingham, called this 1855

structure home. The attraction is restored and elegantly furnished. Special Christmas tours are available.

Harry S. Truman Library
(816) 833-1400
Highway 24 and Delaware

The RLDS Temple

This is the crown jewel for any visit to Independence. You'll find it to be more than a storehouse of books. Within is a museum loaded with photos, documents, films, and artifacts of the life and times of the former president. It also houses a replica of the Oval Office, built just as it was when Truman was president. The library also contains the very office that Truman used during the retirement years. Most importantly, it is the final resting place for the Missouri president and first lady. The Library contains over 14 million manuscripts, 94,000 photographs, 63 miles of film, 700 hours of audio recordings, and an immense collection of 25,000 artifacts. Truman harbored a desire that the Library develop into a center for learning about American history — and that it has truly become.

Jackson County Historical Society
Independence Square
In the Jackson County Courthouse you'll see written on the walls the stories relating the stories of the beginnings of the Oregon and Santa Fe Trails.

1859 Jail Marshall's Home and Museum
(816) 252-1892
217 North Main
Originally built in 1859, this attraction has been restored to its Civil War appearance. Some of its famous residents were William Quantrill and Frank James.

Leila's Hair Museum
(816) 252-HAIR
815 West 23rd Street.
An unusual facility for those who appreciate hair and fine jewelry, the museum claims to possess over 125 wreaths, 750 pieces of jewelry, and artifacts made with human hair before 1900.

1827 Log Courthouse
(816) 325-7111
107 West Kansas
Located in the Independence Square area, the log building, constructed in 1827, can still be viewed.
✪ FREE ADMISSION

National Frontier Trails Center
(816) 325-7575
318 West Pacific
The Santa Fe, Oregon, and California trails are featured in this archive containing information on the trails that settled the western half of the United States. You can also see two authentic 19th century covered wagons.

Pioneer Spring Cabin
(816) 325-7111
Truman Road and Noland
Typical 1850's heartland home. Two room cabin offers sharp contrast to opulent victorian estates. Open April through October 10:00 a.m.-2:00 p.m.
✪ FREE ADMISSION

Reorganized Church of Jesus Christ of Latter Day Saints
(816) 833-1000
River and Walnut Streets
Here you'll find the World Headquarters Complex. It contains the 6,000 seat Auditorium and 1,600 seat Temple. Guided tours and organ recitals are offered.

Vaile Mansion
(816) 325-7111
1500 North Liberty
One of the premier nineteenth century homes in Independence, This 1881 estate contains more than 30 rooms and was the residence of Harvey M. Vaile. Special Christmas tours available.

Satellite Attractions

✇ Sibley
Originally named for Major George C. Sibley, who helped to survey the Sante Fe Trail, the town is located along Highway 24.

Fort Osage
(816) 795-8200
Route 20-E
A Visitor's Center houses exhibits that tell the story of this frontier fort that was in use from 1808 to 1820.

✇ Fleming Park

Missouri Town 1855
(816) 795-8200

The National Frontier Center

East side of Lake Jacomo
A living history village where the past is related through guides, musicians, and crafts people.

🌿 Lone Jack

A blackjack tree near a spring that was used as prairie marking gave birth to the name of this town where a bloody Civil War battle was fought in 1862.

Civil War Museum

(816) 697-2272
State Road 50 and US 50
Site where the Battle of Lone Jack was fought.
◯ FREE ADMISSION

Annual Events

May

• Truman's Anniversary Concert — Symphonic music and virtuoso musicians perform.

June

• Vaile Mansion Strawberry Festival.— Strawberries are the theme behind this Victorian craft and antique exhibition held at the historic Vaile Mansion.

July

• Bingham Waggoner Antique and Craft Fair. More than 140 booths make this an interstate bonanza at the historic estate.

August

• Dawg Days Annual Fair, Craft Show and Flea Market
• Santa-Cal-Gon Days — This four day festival commemorates the famous early American trails used by settlers heading west. There is entertainment along with arts and crafts on Labor day weekend.

September

• Annual Quilt Show

November
- Best Little Arts and Craft Show in Independence — Judge for yourself as more than 130 crafters and artists display their wares.

December
- Spirit of Christmas Past Homes Tour — Experience the thrill of Christmas past when you take part in a festive tour of three of Independence's historic homes.

Shopping and Dining

As you would expect from a rather large community, Independence offers the shopper an exhaustive arena to chose from in antique searching. As far as dinners are concerned, you can eat everything from fast-food to gourmet in just about any location.

In Conclusion

For further information contact:
Independence Tourism Dept
111 East Maple
Independence, MO 64050
1-800-748-7323
WebSite at
http:\\www.ci.independence.mo.us

Tips

✔ Independence is loaded with good roadside signs to find the major exhibits.

✔ Much ground can be covered in the downtown Historic Square region. Parking is available, but expect the customary heavy traffic at certain times of the day.

✔ At the Hill Park Cemetery on 23rd Street, you'll find the grave of Frank James.

66 Most people tell us that if they had known there was so much to see and do in Independence, they would have allowed more time. Many do take additional time and stay over or plan a return visit. From the legacy of pioneers and presidents there is a wealth of things to see and do here. 99

—Cathy Offutt
Volunteer Coordinator
City of Independence

Jefferson City
"A Capitol Place to Visit"

Location

Located 28 miles from Interstate 70 at the crossroads of Highways 54 and 50 in Cole County.

History

Missouri's first Assembly met in St. Louis in 1820, then later in nearby St. Charles. A five-man commission was appointed to come up with a capital along the Missouri River. It's amazing how close Cote Sans Dessein, in Callaway County, was to becoming the site for Missouri's first capital. But land speculators on the south side of the river persevered in landing the site at the current location in Cole County.

On December 21, 1821, the city of Jefferson was selected as the site of the capital. Major Elias Bancroft platted the site in 1822. In May of

Missouri State Capitol

1823, funds were expended to construct a house of government, but it wasn't until 1826 that the Missouri legislature moved from St. Charles to take up the business of governing in Jefferson City.

In 1839 when the city was formally incorporated, the population was just a little under 1,200. By 1855 the advent of the railroad through the city ensured its growth. However, the population did not increase during the Civil War years because Governor Claiborne Jackson removed this pro-Southern seat of government to Neosho.

Today, the view of the majestic Capitol when approaching from the north along Highway 54 is an affirmation of the city's resilience to survive and grow into the twenty-first century.

➡ Getting Started

You can begin your visit at the Jefferson City Chamber of Commerce. The Chamber is located at 213 Adams. From Highway 54, take the East 50/63 Exit, go five blocks and make a left onto Morgan, and then a right onto High Street, and finally a left onto Adams. There is parking there — but it is metered.

Attractions

Most of the historical points of interest are located in the downtown district. You'll find sufficient parking in various areas around the Capitol Building to begin your day trip.

State Capitol Building
(573) 751-4127
Downtown

The Capitol building that can be seen as one approaches Jefferson City along Highway 54 was built following the great fire of 1911, when lightning struck the dome and completely leveled the second home of the Missouri Legislature. The first Capitol was also destroyed by fire in 1837. Tradition has it that this initial disaster was the result of a Senator leaving a fire unattended in his hearth.

Completed in 1918, the four-story Capitol is home to both houses of the Missouri legislature. Your tour of the Jefferson Landing complex should commence here. If you enter the Capitol Building at the first story entrance, you'll see a round desk under the grand stairway. There you'll find guides who will provide you with all of the necessary information to tour the building and its nearby attractions. You have the choice between taking your own self-paced tour or getting a guided tour from one of the guides. The guided tour is conducted every half-hour, with a maximum of sixty people.
✪ FREE ADMISSION

The Capitol is a bee hive of activity, especially when the legislature is in session. On the fourth floor are three galleries—three for the House and one for the Senate — from which you can witness history in the making.

The Capitol also houses many works of art. Murals by the nationally famous Thomas Hart Benton and N. C. Wyeth await the visitor. The building also contains the State Museum, which offers two separate themes. On one side are historical artifacts including Civil War flags, period clothing, the bell from the U.S.S. Missouri, and a model of the nationally famous battleship. The other side of the museum portrays exhibits on fish and animal wildlife in Missouri. One other interesting exhibit in the natural resource side is a miniature model of an authentic mining shaft.

Missouri Veterans Memorial

Located just across the street from the Capitol Building are the memorial and statue of Thomas Jefferson. There you'll enjoy strolling along the walk that contains plaques commemorating all of the wars that Missouri's sons and daughters have participated in.

Governor's Mansion
(573) 751-7929
100 Madison

This 1871 landmark offers further described tours. Don't miss the mansion gardens on your way. Enter the mansion through the iron gates on Madison Street. At the front door you'll be greeted by a guide in period costume who will show you where to begin your self-guided tour of the first floor.
○ Open Tuesday and Thursday only. Closed during August

Supreme Court Building
Another place of interest just across the street from the Capitol is the State Supreme Court Building. Overlooked by many tourists, the building is also open for a self-guided tour through its many court facilities.

Jefferson Landing Historic Site
As you descend the hill towards the river, you'll go by the restored Christopher Maus House and Union Hotel. Finally, at the end of the street you'll find Lohman's Landing. Here you'll find an excellent museum full of original artifacts and dioramas depicting the evolution of the Capitol and the early days in Jefferson City.
○ FREE ADMISSION

Cole County Historical Society Museum
(573) 635-1850
109 Madison Street
This museum is located just across

the street from the Governor's Mansion. Special displays include inaugural ball gowns.

Satellite Attractions

🌿 Westphalia

This town was orignally settled in 1835 by a group of Westphalian families from Germany. You'll find it located south along Highway 63.

Westphalia Historical Society Museum and Town
(573) 455-2250
Main Street and downtown area
An 1835 German-Catholic community with many older homes still standing.

Special Tours

For further information about touring the Jefferson Landing Complex or Capitol, contact:
Capitol Tours, Capitol Building Room B2
Jefferson City, MO 65101

Annual Events

March
• Annual Ice Show — Local skating talent takes to the ice.

July
• July 4th Downtown Celebration
• Cole County Fair

September
• Fall Festival and Crafts Fair — At Cole County Fairgrounds
• Capital Jazzfest

October
• Hartsburg Pumpkin Festival
• River Rendezvous Festival

November
• St. Peter's Craft Show

December
• Annual Capital City Speed Skating Championship
• Christmas in the Capital — Candlelight tours of the Govenor's Mansion highlight this event.
• Annual Christmas Parade

Shopping and Dining

If history, government, nature and art are not enough to fill your desires, you'll find a shopper's paradise in nearby downtown Jefferson City. Craft and antiques shops, along with clothing stores will offer more than an ample opportunity to pick up that 'bargain deal.' If that doesn't suffice, you're not far from the Capital Mall.

In Conclusion

For further information contact:
Jefferson City Convention and Visitors Bureau
PO Box 776
Jefferson City, MO 65102
(800) 769-4183
FAX: (573) 634-3805
Web Site: www.jchamber.org
E-mail: cvb1@jcchamber.org

Govenor's Mansion

Tips

✔ If you are planning a group outing of greater than a dozen individuals, you will need to make reservations for guided tours at the Capitol.

✔ A very popular activity in Jefferson City is to visit the Central Dairy facility for some of the best ice cream for miles around.

✔ Some sound advice for those wishing to visit the Jefferson Landing complex:

✔ Saturdays and Sundays are the slowest days during the summer months.

✔ Expect to see more than a hundred visitors on week days. However, with so much to see spread out over such a large area, the crowds should not prove to be a great hindrance. This is not the case during the spring when up to a thousand people can visit in a single day. This is due to the abundance of school groups coming to town along with others wishing to see their tax dollars at work.

> 66 Perched on a bluff overlooking the Missouri River, Jefferson City's skyline is dominated by its crown jewel, the magnificent domed Capitol Building. The majestic architecture and the renowned artwork of famous Missourians like Thomas Hart Benton which is housed in this hub of activity, have earned Missouri's capitol a reputation as one of the most beautiful in the nation, an opinion which is confirmed by the thousands of visitors who come to visit every year. History, art, and architectural beauty are abundant in this center of state government. The 1871 Governor's Mansion is resplendent with elegance, and is considered one of the most authentic and carefully researched examples of the Renaissance Revival period in the United States.
>
> For nature lovers, the Runge Nature Center offers indoor displays as well as walking trails. In addition to our historical heritage, Jefferson City offers visitors a lovely downtown, a selection of antique and gift shops, beautiful rolling hills, friendly hospitality, and a warm, relaxing atmosphere that will make visitors want to return again and again. 99
>
> —*Kathy Lou Toler*
> *Executive Director*
> *Jefferson City Convention and Visitors Bureau*

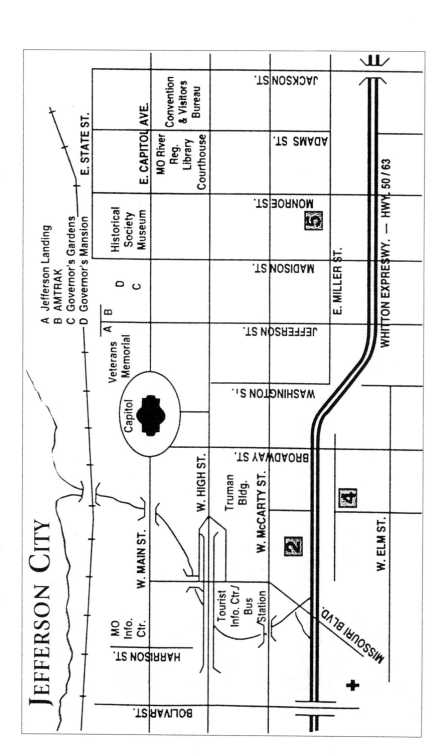

JEFFERSON CITY

A Jefferson Landing
B AMTRAK
C Governor's Gardens
D Governor's Mansion

E. STATE ST.

E. CAPITOL AVE.

Convention & Visitors Bureau

MO River Reg. Library Courthouse

JACKSON ST.

ADAMS ST.

Historical Society Museum

MONROE ST.

MADISON ST.

E. MILLER ST.

JEFFERSON ST.

WASHINGTON St.

WHITTON EXPRESWY. — HWY. 50 / 63

Veterans Memorial

Capitol

W. HIGH ST.

BROADWAY ST.

Truman Bldg.

W. McCARTY ST.

W. MAIN ST.

W. ELM ST.

MO. Info. Ctr.

Tourist Info. Ctr./ Bus Station

HARRISON ST.

MISSOURI BLVD.

BOLIVAR ST.

Kansas City
"A City of Surprises"

Location
Located at the western most part of Interstate 70.

History
Kansas City became an early thoroughfare for travelers heading West along the Oregon, California and Santa Fe Trails.

The area that was to become Kansas City was established in 1821 as a trading post by an agent of the American Fur Company, Francois Chouteau.

By the time Jackson County was formed in 1826, settlers had already begun to congregate in the area with the arrival of riverboats and wagon trains. In the beginning, Independence, being closer to the Sante Fe Trail, became the county seat.

In 1832 John Calvin McCoy built a store to meet the needs of those heading to the West, and also to cash in on the overflow from Independence. The next year he platted the town of Westport. With an ever-increasing influx of merchants, Westport in time rivaled nearby

Kansas City Jazz

J.C. Nichol's Memorial Fountain at Country Club Plaza

Independence for prominence.

In 1838 Chouteau's settlement, which had been called West Port's Landing, was purchased by the Kansas Town Company and renamed Kansas.

The influx of travelers heading along the Sante Fe Trail, along with a growing number of steamboats venturing the Missouri River added greatly to the population of the frontier boom town. Commerce was increased by the traders returning from the Southwest laden with gold and goods to sell or trade.

In 1850, the "Town of Kansas" was incorporated. In 1853 the "Town of Kansas" was charted by the Missouri legislature as the "City of Kansas".

The abundance of Southern sympathizers brought turmoil to Kansas City long before the guns of Fort Sumter. They clashed with an equally zealous group of abolitionists who resided just across the Missouri River in the Free State of Kansas. The years of the Civil War saw much bloodshed as Missouri "Bushwhackers" and Kansas "Red-Legs" Jayhawks battled for supremacy.

Following the war and the advent of the railroad, Kansas City experienced unbridled growth. As Missouri cattle trails were closed, herds were driven to the Kansas cow towns near the tracks. When the 1878 Union Depot was constructed, it was the second largest in the world. With the addition of major bridges and railroad tracks, Kansas City quickly became the transportation hub for the region.

Today the city continues its dominant influence in the area of transportation and growth with industry and culture now the primary catalysts for any increase in Kansas City's population.

➥ Getting Started

The Convention and Visitors Bureau of Greater Kansas City operates the Kansas City Visitor Information Center on the Country Club Plaza. It is open seven days a week at 222 W. 47th Street, across from FAO Schwarz.

The Missouri Tourism Office is located along Interstate 70 east of Kansas City in the vicinity of the Truman sports complex. Here you can get brochures and maps of the KC area. Just take the east Blue Ridge exit and go to your right. You'll see the one story cement building on your right.

Attractions

✦ Civic

Kansas City is home to a variety of entertainment. The following are some of the civic attractions in the metro area.

Board of Trade

(816) 753-7500
4800 Main
Want to see how your dividends are earned? You can for free from the Observation Deck.

Cave Spring Interpretive Center

(816) 358-2283
8701 Gregory at Blue Ridge Blvd
A nature and cultural exhibit.

City Market

(816) 842-1271
5th Street & Grand
Visit the Midwest's largest farmer's market.

Country Club Plaza

(816) 753-0100
47th Street to Ward Parkway
More than 180 shops to explore in prime 1920's architecture.

Crown Center

(816) 274-8444
25th and Grand
The Hyatt Regency Crown Center Hotel and the Westin Crown Center Hotel are the cornerstones of this 85 acre complex of over 100,00 square feet of stores, shops, entertainment facilities and restaurants. Your kids will enjoy Kaleidoscope, a free creative workshop for kids ages 5-12.

Federal Reserve Bank Visitors Center

(816) 881-2200
925 Grand
Learn all about how the government makes money.
✪ FREE ADMISSION

Downtown Kansas City Skyline

Hallmark Visitors Center
(816) 274-5672
25th and Pershing Road,
Crown Center
Self-guided tours show you how
all of those cards you buy are
made.
✪ FREE ADMISSION

Kansas City Zoological Gardens
(816) 871-5700
Interstate 435 and 63rd Street
Animals and exhibits equate to
education and fun for all ages.
✪ FREE ADMISSION

Kelly's Westport Inn
(816) 753-9193

500 Westport Road
Once a store operated by Daniel
Boone's grandson today is a
popular "saloon."

Hoesch Marion Roussel Visitor's Center
(816) 966-4253
10245 Marion Park Drive
Learn all about pharmaceutical
manufacturing. Open by appointment only.

National Archives
(816) 926-6272
2312 East Bannister Road
Everything you need to dig up
your Midwestern roots. You may

want to check with them for instructions prior to visiting.

✤ Entertainment

Kansas City offers a wide variety of educational and recreational opportunities.

Missouri Town 1855

(816) 795-8200
East Side of Lake Jacomo in Blue Springs. An old town has been reconstructed as a backdrop for education and fun.

The Blue Room

(816) 474-2929
1600 East 18th Street
A new club attached to the Kansas City Jazz Museum which contains jazz memorabilia.

Worlds of Fun and Oceans of Fun

(816) 454-4545
I-435
Who said daytrips couldn't be fun — and wet. This water theme park will certainly cool your tired daytrip feet. Side by side amusement parks provide thrills for all ages.

✤ Homes

Along with its modern image, Kansas City has managed to preserve much of its rich heritage.

Alexander Majors House

(816) 333-5556

8201 State Line Road
Visit the 1856 residence of one of the founders of the Pony Express and a lifetime friend of Buffalo Bill.

Thomas Hart Benton Home and Studio State Historic Site

(816) 931-5722
3616 Belleview
Many of the famous artist's works are on display here as well as the original furnishings.

Harris Kearney Home

(816) 561-1821
4000 Baltimore Avenue
Venture to the oldest standing brick home in Kansas City.

John Wornall House Museum

(816) 444-1858
146 W. 61st Street Terrace
This 1858 residence was used as a field hospital during the Civil War.

✤ Museums

If artifacts and exhibits are your cup of tea, try one of these fine museums to quench your thirst.

American Royal Museum and Visitor Center

(816) 221-9800
1701 American Royal Court
Here you'll experience hands-on displays pertaining to agri-business.

Crown Center Complex

Arabia Steamboat Museum
(816) 471-4030
400 Grand, City Market
Two-hundred tons of excavated
cargo from a riverboat that sank
in 1856 are displayed.

Kansas City Jazz Museum
(816) 474-8463
1616 East 18th Street
An interactive museum which
showcases Kansas City's jazz.

Black Archives of Mid-America
(816) 483-1300
2033 Vine Street
African-American history in
Missouri is on display there.

Historic Depot Museum
(816) 761-6271
1205 Jones Street
A restored Kansas City Southern
Station.

Kansas City Fire Museum
(816) 474-0200
1019 Cherry
This turn-of-the-century fire station
houses fire fighting exhibits.
✪ Call for hours

**Kansas City Museum
and Planetarium**
(816) 483-8300
3218 Gladstone Blvd
Displays range from the history of

yesteryear to the technology of the future.

Kemper Museum of Contemporary Art and Design
(816) 561-4852
4420 Warwick Avenue
These galleries laden with art treasures are sure to please all ages.
❂ FREE ADMISSION

Negro Leagues Baseball Museum
(816) 221-1920
18th and Vine
The era of early black baseball is preserved and exhibited.

Nelson-Atkins Museum of Art
(816) 751-1278
4525 Oak Street
Over 30,000 world-wide artifacts, paintings, and statues from ancient history to the present.

Save A Connie
(816) 421-3401
480 Richards Road
An airline museum with exhibits and films.

Toy and Miniature Museum
(816) 333-2055
5235 Oak Street
A 1911 restored mansion houses more than 50,000 small collectibles, antique doll houses and furnishings.

Bruce R. Watkins Cultural Heritage Center
(816) 923-6226
3700 Blue Parkway
An African-American museum and gallery.

Theater
Kansas City is home to a number of fine theatrical establishments. The following are a list of the major facilities and their phone number for further information.
- **American Heartland Theatre** (816) 842-9999
- **Coterie Theatre** (816) 474-6552
- **Folly Theatre** (816) 474-4444
- **Kansas City Symphony** (816) 471-0400
- **Lyric Opera** (816) 471-7344
- **Midland Theatre** (800) 710-7788
- **Missouri Repertory Theatre** (816) 276-2700
- **Starlight Theatre** (816) 363-7827

Satellite Attractions
Kansas City is surrounded by several areas with worthwhile attractions to see.

❧ Belton
Platted in 1871, this town is located south along Highway 71.

Belton Historical Museum
(816) 322-3977
512 Main Street
Truman memorabilia and burial sites of Carrie Nation and Dale Carnegie.

🌿 **Blue Springs**
Located east along I-70.

Dillingham-Lewis House
(816) 229-2659
15th and Main Streets
A turn-of-the-century home to tour. Open 2nd Wednesday of each month 1-4 p.m or by special appointment.

🌿 **Excelsior Springs**
Located 20 minutes north of Kansas City, this community contains 11 natural springs and historical attractions including the Hall of Waters, the 1888 Elms Hotel, and the 1861 Watkins Woolen Mill. Call (816) 630-6161 for further information about these and other attractions.

🌿 **Grandview**
This town is located south along Interstate 435.

Truman Farmhouse
(816) 254-2720
12301 Blue Ridge Blvd
The Harry S. Truman farm from the age of 22-33. He served as a farmer from 1906-1917. Open during the summer months or call for special tour arrangements.

🌿 **Hodge Park**

Shoal Creek Living History Museum
(816) 792-2655
Highway 152, 7000 NE Barry Rd.
A recreated 19th century village with tours and special events year round.

🌿 **Kearney**
This satellite attraction is located north along Interstate 35.

Jesse James Farm and Museum
(816) 628-6065
21216 Jesse James Farm Road
The birthplace of one of this country's most famous outlaws.

🌿 **Kingsville**
Located 30 miles southeast of Lee's Summit along Highway 50.

Powell Gardens
(816) 697-2600
US 50
A gardeners delight. Several gardens to tour and a variety of classes are offered. Call for more information.

🌿 **Liberty**
The seat for Clay County was organized in 1822 and today is located north along Interstate 35.

For more information call Liberty Area Chamber of Commerce (816) 781-5200.

Harry S. Truman Sports Complex

Clay County Historical Society Museum
(816) 792-1849
14 North Main
An 1877 drugstore houses artifacts of the past.

Jesse James Bank Museum
(816) 781-4458
103 North Water Street
Jesse took money out of the original vault, but left lots of memorabilia.

Liberty Jail Visitor's Center
(816) 781-3188
216 North Main Street
Joseph Smith was once a prisoner here in 1838 and 1839.

Lightburne Hall
(816) 781-5567
301 North Water Street
The 1852 home of Major Lightburne. This is a private residence.

William Jewell College
(816) 781-7700
500 College Hill
William Jewell was selected as a college in 1849. It is now a nationally ranked liberal arts college. Jewell Hall located on the campus was occupied by Union troops during the Civil War. Many buildings on campus are listed on the National Historic Register.

"Shuttlecocks" at the Nelson Atkins Museum of Art

❦ Lone Jack

Receiving its name from a blackjack tree near an active spring that served as a prairie landmark, this historic town of the Civil War is located east along Highway 50.

Civil War Museum

(816) 566-2272
Bynum Road
Civil War history is displayed in infirmative exhibitions.
❂ FREE ADMISSION

❦ Smithville

Located north on Highway 169.

Smithville Lake

Woodhenge
(816) 532-0803
This site contains an ancient Indian natural calendar.

❦ Weston

This small town was established in 1837 by Joseph Moore. It is located north along State Route 45.

Price-Loyles House

(816) 640-2383
718 Spring Street
The Boone family home of 1857.
❂ Group tours are welcome

Weston Historical Museum
(816) 386-2977
601 Main Street
Platte County history is displayed.
✪ FREE ADMISSION

Special Tours

Carriage Rides on the Plaza
(816) 531-2673
500 Nichols Road
Take a horse drawn carriage tour
of the Country Club Plaza.

Kansas City Trolley
(816) 221-3399
Runs a continous loop through
KC's main corridor seven days a
week, March through December.

Annual Events

Something for everyone! Please
call for time, location and date. For
more information call 1-800-767-
7700.

February
- RV & Outdoor Show
- Kansas City Boat Show
- Ground Hog Run
- Treasures of Nature Art Show
- Flower, Lawn and Garden Show
- Cabin Fever Quilt Show
- Kansas City Blues Society Mardi Gras Club Crawl
- Remodeling Show
- Police Circus
- Buck Buchanan Sports Festival
- [a] Lake of the Ozarks Boat Show

- Midwest Card Collectors Show

March
- Greater Kansas City Auto Show Big 12 Conference Men's Post-Season Basketball Tournament
- Home Show
- St. Patrick's Day Parade
- Brookside St. Patrick's Day Warm-up Parade
- Snake Saturday
- Gem & Mineral Show
- Johnson County RV Show

April
- Designer's Showhouse
- Greater Kansas City Day
- Worlds of Fun Season Opens
- Home Builders Association of Greater Kansas City Spring Homes Tour
- Spring Herb and Plant Show
- Folk Art Festival
- Kansas City Indian Market and Southwest Showcase

May
- St. Luke's Classic Golf Tourn.
- Abdallah Shrine Rodeo
- Brookside Art Annual
- Truman Week
- Southwest Boulevard Cinco de Mayo Celebration
- Latin American Cinco de Mayo Parade
- Heart of America Barbershop Show
- Historic Preservation Week
- Polski Day
- Blue Devil Cook-Off/Sunflower BBQ Championship
- Twin City Invitational Rodeo

- Oregon Trail Conestoga Days
- Haskell Indian National University Commencement Pow Wow
- Oceans of Fun Grand Opening

June
- Jazz Lovers Pub Crawl
- Old Fashioned Days
- Family Fun Fests
- Cooporate Woods Jazz Festival
- Highland Games
- Lost Trail Root Beer Days
- Juneteenth Celebration
- Great Lenexa BBQ Battle/ Kansas State Barbeque Contest
- Old Shawnee Days
- Crawfish Fiesta
- Cole Younger Days
- Trinity Hospital Hill Run
- Strawberry Festival
- Bullwhacker Days
- Jazzoo
- Jaguar Concours d'Elegance
- Settlers Day
- Gladstone Summertime Blues Fest
- 39th Street West Fest
- Lost Arts Festival
- Downtown Overland Park Days

July
- Independence Day at the Truman Library
- Heart of America Shakespeare Festival
- Kansas City Blues and Jazz Festival
- Water Gardens Tour
- Reggaefest

- Independence Day at Missouri Town 1855 and Fort Osage
- Kansas City Indian Club Pow Wow
- Jaycees Pro Rodeo & Wild West Extravaganza

December
- Christmas on the River
- Disney on Ice
- "A Christmas Carol"
- "Nutcracker"
- Missouri Town 1855 Christmas Celebration
- Spirits of Christmas Past Historic Homes Tour
- Shawnee Indian Mission Christmas Open House
- Kansas City Symphony Family Holiday Concern

Shopping and Dining

If you've something in mind, chances are you'll find it, and many other buyables, here in Kansas City. And for eating pleasure, just call all of your relatives back East and tell them about eating prime rib and special barbecue sauce in the beef capital of the world.

In Conclusion

For further information contact:
Convention and Visitors Bureau of
Greater Kansas City
1100 Main Street Suite 2550
Kansas City, MO 64105
(800) 767-7700 or (816) 221-5242

Kansas City

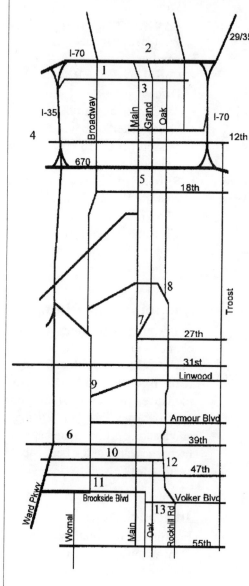

1. City Market
2. Arabia Steamboat Museum
3. Kansas City Fire Museum
4. American Royal Museum
5. Federal Reserve Bank Visitors Center
6. Thomas Hart Benton Home
7. Crown Center
8. Hallmark Visitors Center
9. Kelly's Westport Inn
10. Harris Kearney Home
11. Country Club Plaza
12. Nelson-Atkins Museum of Art
13. Toy and Miniature Museum

66 A city full of fountains and majestic tree-lined boulevards, Kansas City offers endless entertainment opportunities. The Country Club Plaza recreates the flavor of Europe and its sparkling fountains and majestic towers, while Hallmark Cards' Crown Center provides entertainment and shopping atmosphere.

Kansas City is famous for its delicious steaks and mouth-watering barbecue, but it also offers some of the finest history and art museums in the country, including the Nelson-Atkins Museum of Art, and the Arabia Steamboat Museum.

The city recently unveiled the newest jewel in its crown — the Museums at 18th and Vine. This new cultural attraction includes the Kansas City Jazz Museum, the Negro Leagues Baseball Museum and the renovated Gem Theater Cultural and Performing Arts Center.

The expanded Kansas City Zoo offers a selection of newly-constructed world class exhibits. Professional symphony, ballet, opera and theatrical performances are offered throughout the year.

Professional baseball, football, soccer, hockey, and tennis teams play in state-of-the-art facilities throughout the year. Visitors always enjoy Kansas City's famous jazz, which can be heard in numerous venues.

A trip to Kansas City offers so much to discover, you'll wish your daytrip was a weektrip! 99

—Maxine Odell
Director of Public Relations/Publications
Convention and Visitors Bureau of Greater Kansas City

CVB

Lake of the Ozarks
"A Water Wonderland"

Location

Located along Highway 5 and 54 in Miller, Morgan, and Camden counties. Approximately 165 miles from Kansas City, 175 miles from St. Louis and 80 miles from Springfield.

History

The Lake of the Ozarks is more of a region than an actual town. It is composed of three counties and several towns bordering the shoreline of the massive lake that was created with the Bagnell Dam project in 1929. Over one million cubic yards of earth and 73,000 cubic yards of rock were excavated in the dam's installation. Today more than 1,150 miles of shoreline are home to residents in the neighboring towns.

In Miller County, there is Lakeland and Lake Ozark; in Camden County you have Osage Beach, Camdenton, Linn Creek and Greenview; in Morgan County you have Gravois Mills, Laurie, and Versailles.

Before the construction of Bagnell Dam, the area was a wooded, hilly region whose first inhabitants were bands of Osage Indians. Later, as settlers

Willmore Lodge

began to move in, towns sprang up along travel and postal routes.

Today the Lake of the Ozarks region is full of trails crisscrossing the forests in the exact location that the original Indians used. In some locations are what are called thong trees. Thong trees were originally bent in some unique fashion to mark the nearby location of a spring, a cave, salt licks, or even groves with medicinal herbs. The pioneers sometimes called them "water trees" since they many times pointed to a source of water. Another name was "buffalo tree" because squaws aired out their buffalo hides on the trees.

➡ Getting Started

The Lake of the Ozarks is served by five Chamber of Commerce Offices. Start your visit by calling or visiting any Chamber listed below for further information.

Lake Area Chamber of Commerce
1-800-451-4117— Serving the East Side: Osage Beach, Lake Ozark, Horseshoe Bend, North Shore, Linn Creek and Kaiser.

The chamber is housed in the Willmore Lodge Property a historic log building built in 1930 for Union Electric officials as they came to oversee progress on the dam.

The 6,700 square foot structure was constructed from White Pine Logs, brought into the area by rail from northwestern United States logging companies. No nails were used, pegs held all the logs together. The stone for the patios and fireplace were quarried from local area quarries.

The Chamber occupies a section of the building allowing members and visitors a historical and unique setting in which to conduct chamber business.

The visitor center portion of the building features high tech equipment for visitors wanting information on the area for vacationing, relocation or retirement.

Lake of the Ozarks West Chamber of Commerce—
(573) 374-5500 —Serving the Hwy 5 Area: Gravois Mills, Laurie, Sunrise Beach, Hurricane Deck and Greenview.

Eldon Chamber of Commerce
(573-392-3742—The Eastern Gateway to the Lake of the Ozarks

Versailles Chamber of Commerce
(573) 378-4401— The Western Gateway to the Lake of the Ozarks

Lake of the Ozarks Chamber of Commerce
1-800-769-1004—Serving the Big Niangua & the Little Niangua, Camdenton Area.

Ha Ha Tonka

Attractions

Big Surf
(573) 346-6111
Highway 54 and Highway Y
Okay, maybe you need a break
from a long day of shopping. This
is just the place to cool your feet
and relax a bit.

House of Butterflies
(573) 348-0088
Route 2, Box 3192, Hwy. 54
Osage Beach
Colorful living butterflies displayed in their own habitat to
welcome you.

Miner Mike's
(573) 348-2126
Highway 54 in Osage Beach

You'll find rides, games, and
amusements for the whole family.

Ha Ha Tonka State Park
(573) 346-2986
5 miles southwest of Camdenton
The focal point of the park is the
remains of a turn-of-the-century
castle originally built by Robert
McClure Snyder, a wealthy Kansas
City businessman who hired
Scottish stonemasons to begin
constructing the enormous estate
in 1905.

Lake of the Ozark State Park
(573) 346-2500
Highway 54 to State Road A
Recreational fun includes Ozark
Caverns, The Angle's Shower, and
Visitor Center.

The Shrine of St. Patrick
Located on O Road in Laurie is a church built in 1878 by Irish immigrants to the area, the solidly built structure is composed of native rock from a nearby quarry. On its earthen floor are pews manufactured from local trees.

Lake Museums

Before Bagnell Dam was built much of the areas history is preserved in three county museums. For more information call 1-800-FUN LAKE.

Camden County Museum
(573) 346-7191
Route V just off U.S. Hwy. 54
Housed in the former Linn Creek School you will find classrooms devoted to particular themes from archives to a weaving room. Lots of history and rock collections to be seen at this attraction.

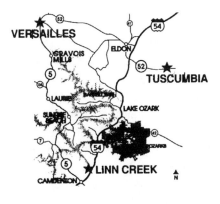

Miller County Historical Society Museum
(573) 392-5206
West Highway 52
Tuscumbia
Housed in the old Anchor Mill building you will find displays portraying early folk life of the early settlers in the area. Indian relics, crafts, schools and other early historical artifacts are on display.
✪ Free Admission.

Morgan County Historical Museum
(573) 378-5556
120 North Monroe Street
Located in Versailles in the Martin Hotel. The hotel is a 100 year old landmark and was a regular stage stop between Jeffersonville and Springfield. Within the facility you will find some twenty-eight rooms furnished in various themes ranging from a chapel room to a school room. Preserved in the lobby of the hotel is the an eight-day Seth Thomas wall clock and a keyboard with keys displayed behind the original hotel desk.

Natural Attractions

Caverns
With a constant temperature of 56 degrees, these underground wonders can be enjoyed most of the year.

- **Bridal Cave** (573) 346-2676 in Camdenton reportedly holds the record for the number of underground weddings.
- **Jacob's Cave** (573) 378-4374 in Versailles claims to the be the largest in the area.
- **Ozark Spring Cave** (573) 765-5223 in Richland, is a shelter cave.
- **Fantasy World Caverns** is located 3/4 mile off Hwy 54, 7 miles East of Bagnell Dam, 1 mile West of Jct 52 and 54. Used by man and animals for thousands of years. Inside you will find four Indian Burial sites.

Entertainment

There are several family oriented country music shows at the Lake of the Ozarks region.

Lee Mace's Ozark Opry
(573) 348-2270
Main Street Music Show
(573) 348-9500
Kin Folks Music Shows
(573) 346-6797
Ozark Jubilee
(573) 348-8989
Jerry Prunty
(573) 302-0023
Ozark Opry
(573) 348-2560

Special Tours

Casino Pier
Excursion Boat Fun Cruises
(573) 356-2020

The boat runs daily from Casino Pier located near Bagnell Dam.
✪ Sightseeing and meals

Air Lake Aviation
(573) 348-4469
Highway 54 and KK
Charter flights and aircraft rental are available for viewing the lake from the air.

Tropic Island Cruises
(573) 348-0083
✪ Sightseeing and meals.

Tom Sawyer Excursion Boat
(573) 365-3300 —
✪ Sightseeing

Annual Events

For a complete listing of annual events, dates and further information call 1-800-Fun Lake.

March
- Annual Lake of the Ozarks Product & Services Show, Lake Expo Center, D Road, Osage Beach.

April
- Annual Marine Dealers Boat show, Marriott's Tan-Tar-A
- Annual Dogwood Music Festival, downtown Camdenton & Camdenton School.
- Taste of Lake of the Ozarks, Stonecrest Mall, Osage Beach.

May
- Annual Magic Dragon Street Meet Car Show held at the Lake Expo Center, Osage Beach.
- Annual Spring Harbor Hop (Poker run on the water).

- First Annual Spring IJSBA Jet Sport Jam held at Linn Creek Campgrounds.
- Memorial Day Fireworks Display — Lodge of the Four Seasons.

June
- Country Craft Show at the Stonecrest Mall in Osage Beach.
- Annual Lions Club Bagnell Dam Gun Show, School of the Osage Middle School, Osage Beach.

July
- Fireworks on the Water, Marriott's Tan-Tar-A Resort, Osage Beach.
- Independence Day Weekend Fireworks Display, Lodge of Four Seasons
- Super Session Classic Rock & Roll Show & Dance
- Annual Heritage Days & Crafts Festival, Jacob's Cave Meadowland

August
- Annual Cruise to the Lake Dam Car Club Show
- Annual Shooters Shootout Boat Race
- Lake of the Ozarks Blues, Hillbilly Fairgrounds, Laurie
- Annual Fall IJSBA Jet Sport Jam, Linn Creek Campgrounds

September
- Cabin Fever Quilt Show, Camden County Museum
- Annual Hillbilly Fair in Laurie
- Mountain Man Rendezvous — Black powder and authentic costumes highlight this event.
- Fall Festival of Color Hot Air Balloon Race — Lots of bal-

Black Powder Rendevouz
Lake Ozark

loons, food and entertainment.
- Mid Missouri Steam and Gas Engine Show — Old tractors and antique cars enhance this event.

October
- Annual Old Thyme Apple Festival
- Annual Eldon Turkey Festival
- Annual Lake of the Ozarks Dixieland Jazz Festival
- "A Christmas Carol", Sunrise Beach Community
- Lake of the Ozarks West Chamber Christmas Parade, Laurie
- Santa Visits Camdenton
- Bluegrass Music Awards

November
- National Oil and Acrylic Painting Exhibit

December
- Eldon Aglo, Downtown
- Annual Lake Lights Festival & Lake Ozark, Osage Beach
- St. Patrick's Church Festival of Lights
- Annual Enchanted Village of Lights

Shopping and Dining

One of the main shopping attractions is the Osage Outlet Mall, with dozens of stores to choose from. The Lake area is also loaded with a full spectrum of dining facilities.

In Conclusion

For further information contact:
Lake of the Ozark Convention and Visitor Bureau
PO Box 98
Osage Beach, MO 65049
(800) 386-5253
Web Site: www.funlake.com

Tips

✔ Come to Ha Ha Tonka State park and walk the trails amid the dogwood in April.

✔ We have numerous miniature golf courses and go-cart tracks. For information call 1-800-386-5253

✔ A number of businesses have boat rentals. Call 1-800-490-8474 for more information.

Central Missouri's *Lake of the Ozarks*

Lexington
"Fields of Valor"

Location
Located east of Kansas City along Highway 24 in Lafayette County.

History
Lexington was founded in 1822. Much of America's early history has touched the small town. From the passing of Lewis and Clark to the later Pony Express, Lexington has been a witness to much of this country's heritage.

National prominence came to the small town in 1861 when Missouri State Guards under Confederate General Sterling Price defeated a Union force under the command of Colonel James A. Milligan. This was one of three major battles to be fought in Missouri during the course of the war.

➡ Getting Started
You can begin your trip by stopping by the Lexington Chamber of Commerce located at 817 Main Street or the Lexington Tourism Bureau located at the back of the 1830 Log House Museum at the corner of Main and Broadway.

Attractions
There are more than 119 homes and buildings listed on the National Register of Historic Places in Lexington. Many are open for tours by appointment.

Anderson House
The 1853 home of Colonel Oliver Anderson is located adjacent to the Lexington Battlefield and was used as a hospital during the battle.

Lafayette County Courthouse
This 1847 built courthouse is reportedly the oldest acting courthouse still operating west of the Mississippi. You can still see a Confederate cannonball embedded in one of its columns.

Lexington Battlefield State Historic Site and Visitor's Center
(816) 259-4654
North 13th Street
You can still see the trenching from this epic 1861 battle of the Civil war. The Center offers exhibits and narrated video. The

battlefield tour is self-guided, and picnicking and fishing facilities are available.

Lexington Historical Museum
(816) 259-6313
112 South 13th Street
This museum is housed in an 1846 former Presbyterian Church. Artifacts and photos highlight its many displays.

1830 Log House Museum
(816) 259-4711
Main and Broadway
Located along the famous Sante Fe Trail, this restored log residence overlooking the river has been filled with period furnishings.

Madonna of the Trail
A statue erected by the Daughters of the American Revolution commemorates the route taken by the early settlers from Maryland to California.

Wentworth Military Academy
(816) 259-2221
18th and Washington
Established in 1880, the military academy still earns a highly esteemed reputation. Tours can be arranged by appointment.

Satellite Attractions

◊ Higginsville
Located south along State Road 213.

Confederate Memorial State Historical Site
(816) 259-4654
One mile north on State Road 20 and 13 — Along with the preserved Old Confederate Soldier's Home, there are more than 115 acres in which to enjoy the outdoors.

Higginsville Depot
(816) 584-6474
2113 Main —
This restored train depot of 1889 houses a museum.
❂ FREE ADMISSION

◊ Richmond
Located north along State Road 13, this town was platted in 1827 and later became the seat for Ray County.

Ray County Historical Society and Museum
(816) 776-2305
901 West Royle
Civil War and Indian artifacts.

Annual Events
June
• Lexington Heritage Days
September
• Battle of Lexington Re-enactment — This occurs only every three years.
• Vintage Homes Tour
December
• Women's Club Holiday Homes Tour
• Christmas Crafts Bazaar

Shopping and Dining

Many shopping opportunities in a place so filled with history, and the Lexington community will not leave you disappointed. There are a number of eating facilities there also.

In Conclusion

For further information contact:
Lexington Tourism Bureau
PO Box 132
Lexington, MO 64067
(816) 259-4711

Mexico
"Discover the Difference"

Location
Located along Highway 54 in Audrain County; 15 minutes north of I-70 and Kingdom City exit.

History
In 1837 Mexico was chosen as the county seat for Audrain County. With rolling plains and fertile fields, the area quickly became known for agricultural production. Very soon, show horses became the pastime of the community and Mexico became known as the "Saddle Horse Capital of the World."

In 1990, with the discovery of massive clay deposits, fireclay manufacturing became the principal industry and the city became known as the "Firebrick Capital of the World".

Since the 1980's Mexico has become home to new, diversified industries while retaining its small town friendliness, values and ambiance.

➠ Getting Started
You will find the Chamber of Commerce Office at the corner of Jackson and Jefferson Streets on the Village Square in Mexico. Follow the "Central Business District" signs.

Attractions

Audrain Historical Society and American Saddle Horse Museum at Graceland
(573) 581-3910
501 South Muldrow Street
1857 Greek Revival home features historical furnishings, and exhibits. Saddle Horse Museum includes equestrian displays. One-room Country School depicts education as it used to be. Newly restored Country Church features "Akron Style" Church from the late 1800's. The grounds include a walking path with gardens featuring flowers and landscaping popular in the 1900's.

Barbary Coast Complex
103 North Coal Street
One of the more eclectic collections of artifacts in the entire state. A truly "must-see-to-believe" exhibit.

Audrain County Historical Museum and the American Saddle Horse Historical Museum

Missouri Military Academy
Campus tours and demonstrations are available at this award winning educational institution. Established in 1898, the home of the Fusiliers, the Academy requires advance reservations for tours.

Presser Hall
Theatrical and musical presentations year round in this restored auditorium at the old Hardin College campus.

Antiques, Collectibles and Art
Mexico is home to numerous small shops and has two antique malls. There is a resident artist, a potter, and an art gallery, "The Vault Gallery" located in the Chamber building exhibits works by local artists.

Special Tours
Step-on guide for bus tours are available. "Also, Discover Mexico" tour tapes available at the Chamber office.

Satellite Attractions

☙ Centralia
Established in 1857, it is located west along State Road 22.
Centralia Historical Society and Chance Gardens
(573) 682-5711
319 East Sneed Street
Turn of the century country house museum with elaborate gardens.

Audrain County
Amish Community
West on State Road 22 to right on YY.

Purchase a map as you enter this farm community with no electrical or telephone lines. Follow the map and side roads for a step back in time . . . horse drawn carriages and farm implements, smiling children and friendly waves from the fields. Stop at the farms with signs indicating "eggs", "bread", etc.

Annual Events

June
- Miss Missouri Scholarship Pageant
- Village Square Craft Fair—sidewalk sales of handmade items
- Clay Day USA
- Antique Auto Show

July
- 4-H Fair and Audrain Agri-business Concert

August
- Audrain County Historical Society Country Fair

September
- MS 150 Bike Tour
- Soybean Festival

October
- Streetmaster Car Show and Brick City Fun Run

Shopping and Dining

You will find everything from "A to Z" at Mexico's three distinct shopping areas: the Village Square, West Plaza and Teal Lake/South Trails. There is a diversified selection of restaurants — Mexican, Chinese, Barbecue, Steaks and Seafood, or plain old home cooking plus fast foods.

In Conclusion

For further information contact:
Mexico Chamber of Commerce
PO Box 56
Mexico, MO 65265-0056
(800) 581-2765
FAX 573 581 6226

66 Celebrations, friendly people, charming small town ambiance ... that's Mexico. We are proud of our beautiful older homes and gracious tree-lined streets. Recall the past with a visit to our quaint village square with its brick sidewalks and park benches — a perfect place to rest and watch small town America at its best. Mexico is also home to great outdoor facilities and beautiful parks.

We at the Chamber can help you to plan a visit tailored to your interests. So come visit us and discover the difference. 99

—Sue Caine
Executive Vice-President
Mexico Area Chamber of Commerce

Moberly
"The Magic City"

Location

Traveling down Interstate 70, exit at U.S. Highway 63 north and Moberly is located 34 miles from Columbia.

History

Moberly's roots go back to vast prairies of grass and to a village called Allen. Near there in the 1860's was the location of tracks for the Chariton and Randolph Railroad and it was the laying of track that invited the settlement along the rail line. Irishman, Patrick Lynch, invited the residents of Allen to move the little village to the location along the track and the town of "Moberly" began. Named after Colonel William Moberly, superintendent of the railroad, Moberly was platted and grew so rapidly it soon became known as the "Magic City."

➡Getting Started

The Moberly Chamber of Commerce building is located at 211 West Reed Street. (660) 263-6070.

Attractions

Moberly Speedway
(660) 263-6070
Highway 24
Call the Chamber for information about weekend racing and other events located on the 3/8 mile oval dirt track.

Randolph County Historical Society
(660) 263-9396
Visit the Society's Railroad Museum located in the Railway Express Agency building. This building is the only original building remaining near the site of the original railroad crossing. Various displays, including caboose and watchman's shanty on the grounds.

Randolph County Historical Center
(660) 263-9396
223 North Clark
General Omar Bradley memorabilia, genealogy, and research is on display.

Fourth Street Theater
(660) 263-9396
Designed by local architect, Luwig Abt has been donated to the society. Live productions and

General Omar Nelson Bradley

movies were held here in the early 1900's

Rothwell Park
(660) 263-6757
Outdoor sports, recreation around two lakes include fishing and paddle boating.

Sugar Creek Lake
(660) 263-6757
Camping, fishing, and hiking are all available options here.

Satellite Attractions

🌿 **Glasgow**
Got its name in 1836 from a man by the name of James Glasgow. The town is located west along State Road 5.

Glasgow Community Museum
(660) 338-2377
402 Commerce
This 1861 church houses historical displays and art.

Lewis Library, Glasgow
(660) 338-2395
4th and Market
This 1866 structure contains a host of artifacts.

Stump Island Park, Glasgow
(660) 338-2377
A Lewis and Clark encampment has petrified stumps.

ὠ Keytesville

This town established in 1830 by the Reverend Mr. James Keyte is located west along Highway 24.

Gen. Streeterling Price Museum
(660) 288-3204
412 Bridge Street
Prized possessions and Indian relics are displayed.

Annual Events

June
- Randolph County Flywheel Reunion — Steam and gasoline engines
- Huntsville Horse Show — Sutliff Stadium

July
- Fireworks in the Park
- Randolph County Fair — Carnival, 4H livestock show; queen contest, etc.

August
- Higbee Fair & Carnival — Higbee

September
- Downtown Association "Duck Race"
- Old Settlers Days and Hobby Fair — Historic Celebration
- Native American Pow Wow — Native American displays, exhibits history in Rothwell Park
- Magic City Piecemakers Quilt Show

November
- Randolph County Craft Show — Held in Municipal Auditorium

December
- Chamber of Commerce Christmas Parade
- Altrusa Holiday Lighting in the Park

Shopping and Dining

You will find downtown and perimeter shopping more than sufficient as well as a good selection of eating facilities. At the junction of 24 and 63 there are large retailers, strip malls, shopping and more food.

In Conclusion

For further information contact:
Moberly Chamber of Commerce
PO Box 602
Moberly, MO 65270
(660) 263-6070
FAX: 660 263 9443
Web Site:
www.moberlymo.com/chamber

❝ Whether Moberly/Randolph County is a destination, or a place to stop and rest on your way, we want you to feel at home. Good restaurants, clean/safe motels, wonderful shopping areas, parks to walk or picnic and much more are available to you for a one hour stay or for many days.

Located centrally between St. Louis and Kansas City, and, only 34 miles from Columbia, Missouri — Moberly is historic, it is modern and very progressive. Good schools/colleges, excellent medical care, fine older homes and new subdivisions blend into a quality of life you will thoroughly enjoy. Recreation . . . sure! Walk, fish, swim, camp or play in Rothwell Park's 447 acres right in the city. Hunt, fish and hike around area lakes or wildlife areas. Turn back the clock as you visit the vast Amish region nearby with shops for baked goods, woodworking and leather.

And, if you are a history buff visit the Railroad Museum and Historical Center of the Randolph County Historical Society. If you have served in the military then the statue of Five Star General of the Armies, Omar Bradley is a must. Located among other service memorials this bronze statue of Bradley recognizes and honors one of Randolph County's famous sons.

Please call the Chamber of Commerce for more information, we will be happy to help you. Best wishes for safe travels and we hope you will stop to visit us in Moberly/Randolph County. ❞

—*J.W. Ballinger, III*
Executive Vice President
Moberly Chamber of Commerce

Rocheport
"The Heart of the Heartland"

Location
Located in Boone County along Interstate 70 at the Rocheport Exit #115. Take exit and go north 2 miles on State Highway BB to town.

History
Despite it's diminuitive size, the town of Rocheport has played a significant role in Missouri's history. The famous Lewis & Clark Expedition of 1804 landed here and recorded observations of what they saw.

Rocheport was founded in 1825. Blessed with a deep, sheltered cove, a reliable ferry and superior roads, Rocheport was easily accessible overland or by river travel. Rocheport grew rapidly, paralleling the development of steamboat transportation. In 1840, Rocheport was the site for the Whig Convention. Thousands of delegates traveled to Rocheport to support William Henry Harrison's campaign.

The Civil War subjected the town to frequent guerilla raids by Confederate and Union troops alike. Despite strong southern sympathies and a week-long occupation in 1864 by Confederate guerilla Bill Anderson, Rocheport was also an important site for "Underground Railroad" activities.

After the war, Rocheport prospered as a business center into the 1800's and 1890's. The Missouri, Kansas and Texas railroad was built through the town in 1892-1893. The only tunnel built on the MKT Line survives today, nearby. Disastrous fires in 1892 and 1922 destroyed some of the original historic buildings. Because of the historic significance of the town, Rocheport was listed on the National Register of Historic Places in 1976.

➡ Getting Started
There is currently no Visitor's Center *per se* in this quiet old community. However, local merchants have a concise Visitor's Brochure with maps to help you find your way. The town's small size and cozy atmosphere, along with free and abundant parking, makes almost any place a good place to start. Central and Third Streets are the two principal

avenues of business, however, there are several fine merchants and points of interest located along Rocheport's side streets.

Attractions

Friends of Rocheport Museum
(573) 698-3701
100 Moniteau Streets
Historical artifacts and photos highlight this attraction.
✪ Open weekend afternoons, spring through fall

Katy Trail State Park
Located at the intersection of Pike and First Streets. Signage will help guide you there.

Called "The Scenic Gateway to the Katy Trail," Rocheport's section of the Katy Trail lives up to its billing. The trail winds between towering bluffs and the mighty Missouri River, make walking or biking a memorable experience. Wildlife and breathtaking natural beauty abound.
✪ Bike rentals, refreshments and parking are available at the trailhead.

MKT Depot
Public restrooms and trail information are available in this replica railroad depot, located at the Katy Trail parking lot.

Railroad Tunnel
The only tunnel built on the MKT Railroad in 1892-93 still stands. The Katy Trail runs through its cool confines just outside Rocheport.

LeBourgeois Winery
Wine-tasting, tours and sales available at this facility, located just north of the I-70/Rocheport Exit #115.

LeBourgeois Winegarden and Bistro
Located one mile north of the I-70/Rocheport exit, along State Highway BB. High atop the bluffs, this outdoor winegarden offers a stunning view of the Missouri River valley. Close by, a new restaurant of unique construction and location complements the inspiring view with fine dining.

Shopping, Dining and Lodging
Rocheport's national reputation for its quality offerings is well-deserved. Explore unique and diverse shops, many of which are located in restored, well-kept 19th century homes and buildings. Sample superb dining and, for an overnight stay, relax in one of the area's world-class Bed and Breakfast facilities. Several lovely old churches and historic landmarks add flavor to this quaint community.

In Conclusion

For more information contact:
Farm Road Antiques
370 N. Roby Farm Road
Rocheport, MO 65279
(573) 698-2206

Tips

✔ If you don't want to bring your own bike along, Bikes are available at Trailside Cafe, Bike Rentals and Sales located next to KATY Trail State Park. Their phone number is (573) 698 -2702 and they offer bike rentals in all sizes.

✔ The tranquil, shaded streets of Rocheport offer visitors convenient avenues to explore this old river town. Park and walk — savor the relaxed movement of time and discover Rocheport for yourself.

✔ Sitting astride Interstate 70, at Exit #115, nearby Missouri River City features antique shops, an antique mall and a superb Bed and Breakfast housed in an Antebellum home.

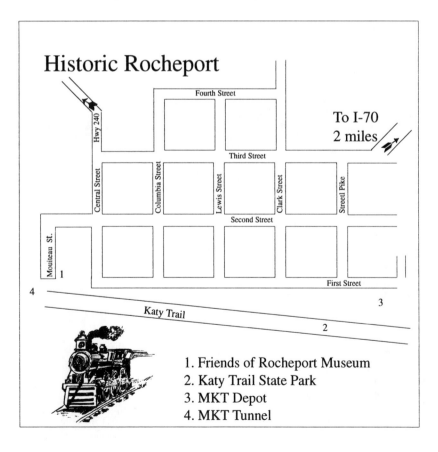

Historic Rocheport

To I-70
2 miles

1. Friends of Rocheport Museum
2. Katy Trail State Park
3. MKT Depot
4. MKT Tunnel

Sedalia
"Queen City of the Prairies"

Location

Located along Highway 50 in Pettis County. Coming from Interstate 70 take the Marshall/Sedalia exit Highway 65 south.

History

Sedalia was founded in 1860 by George Smith. He originally desired to call the town Sedville, but through the encouragement of relatives back East, he chose a name they assured him sounded a bit more cosmopolitan — thus Sedalia was born. A year later, when the Pacific Railroad came through the small town, herds of Texas steers joined a throng of adventurous merchants in creating a boom town in Sedalia.

Cow towns, as they were called, catered to the spending habits of the rugged cowboys. Sedalia, much like Abilene in Kansas, was an oasis for

Activities Along the MKT Trail

Bothwell Lodge

frolicking adventure. The hardy trail riders were usually looking for a cold drink, a hot date, and a night-long card game following their many weeks of driving the herds up the dusty trails through Texas and Oklahoma. Thus, saloons and red light districts were distinct trademarks of the cow towns. Sedalia was no exception.

When the railroad began to branch out closer to the cattle ranches in Texas, and barbed wire blocked the passage of the long-horned steers, the cow towns in Kansas and Missouri began to decline. Sedalia was spared this fate by the removal of the Missouri Kansas and Texas Railroad Division Headquarters from Mokane in Callaway County, to Sedalia.

To reinforce its importance, in 1904, the town was selected as the home of the Missouri State Fair.

Sedalia is the locale from which Scott Joplin, famous ragtime composer, wrote his most popular rag song, *The Maple Leaf Rag*. It was named for the Sedalia-based Maple Leaf Club.

➡ Getting Started

In the summer, you can stop by Sedalia's Visitors Center, a restored railroad caboose car located on South 65. This is closed after Labor Day, but still has an outdoor display with brochures and maps. In off-season, stop by the Sedalia Chamber of Commerce Office at 113 East 4th Street.

Attractions

Downtown Historic District Walking Tour

Stop by the office of the Sedalia Area Chamber of commerce, 113 East Fourth Street, in the Historic Downtown, to receive your free walking tour brochure. Stroll the area learning about the architecture of the buildings and history of the community. Shop the many antique and specialty shops located in the Downtown Historic District.

Pettis County Courthouse and Historical Society Museum

(660) 826-4892
Historic courthouse contains local artifacts and exhibits.
❂ Monday-Friday closed holidays

Scott Joplin International Ragtime Foundation

1-800-827-5295 or
(660) 826-2271
Located across the street from the original Maple Leaf Club, this 4,000 square foot, two story 1800's building is the intended home of a ragtime museum, classroom, recital space and a ragtime store. You will find the finest collection of ragtime music and merchandise available. The Foundation, which holds the annual Scott Joplin Festival, is actively seeking funding for the building's restoration. The Scott Joplin Ragtime Store provides the finest collection of ragtime music and merchandise available. On line Site: http\\scottjoplin.org

Bothwell Lodge State Historic Site

(660) 827-0510
Seven miles north on US 65 stands the former home of John H. Bothwell. Built in sections, the castle-like structure was constructed using native rock from the estate's grounds. Guides conduct tours through the lodge throughout the year. Approximately 180 acres, includes hiking trails, picnicking.
❂ Tours of stone lodge daily —

Sedalia Ragtime Archives

(660) 530-5800
3201 West 16th Street
State Fair Community College Library, Maple Leaf Room. Includes original sheet music, piano rolls, and tapes of interviews with Eubie Blake.

Katy Trail State Park

1-800-827-5295 or
The Missouri-Kansas-Texas railroad tracks were removed and the path converted to the longest rails-to-trails linear park in the U.S. Katy

Trail State Park stretches 233 miles across Missouri with a trailhead just east of Sedalia. This hiking and biking trail showcases some of Missouri's most beautiful scenery.

Katy Depot

The Katy Depot, located at Third and Thompson is the largest depot along the Katy Trail State Park. Renovation started in early 1998, the depot is planned to house a railroad museum.

Paint Brush Prairie Natural Area

(660) 530-5500

This natural landscape area, located nine miles south of Sedalia, captures the historic atmosphere at the time of homesteading. Unique plant species have been restored to the area, encouraging the return of native animals like prairie chickens, upland sandpipers, and Henslow's sparrows. Hiking trails wind throughout the area and visitors are welcome.

The Sedalia Murals

200 South Osage

The murals are located in the Sedalia Municipal Building. They are open for viewing from 8:30 a.m. to 5:00 p.m. Monday through Friday except public holidays. Eric James Bransby, a 20th century American painter, muralist and educator, and an authority on the history and technique of mural

painting, was commissioned in 1976 to execute the Sedalia murals. Our murals mirror Sedalia— a community drawing from the wisdom of the past, and constantly looking with vision to the future.

The Bothwell

Conveniently located in downtown Sedalia at Fourth and Ohio, this historic site is named to the Department of Interior Register of Historic Places. The seven-story building operates as an assisted living facility for the elderly while maintaining its hotel and motel license. Also housed within the hotel are a public restaurant and a beauty-barber shop.

Sedalia Public Library

The first library to receive an Andrew Carnegie Grant in the state of Missouri, the structure was dedicated in 1901. Boasting marble floors, open fireplaces, white oak woodwork, it is made of terra cotta and Carthage stone.

Satellite Attractions

᭵ Tipton

The town named for Tipton Sealey, who donated the land in 1858, is located east along Highway 50.

Maclay Home

(660) 433-2101

Highway B

Tour this seminary for girls that was built in 1858.

῎ Warsaw

An important shipping point along the Osage River, this town became the seat for Benton County in 1837. Today it is located south along Highway 65.

Benton County Museum

(660) 438-7462
700 Benton Street
An 1886 School House is open for tours.

J and S Old West Museum

(660) 438-2631
1038 East Main
Enjoy antique saddles and Indian artifacts.
❂ FREE ADMISSION

Special Tours

Circle tours brochures highlighting rural communities within a 60 mile radius of Sedalia and walking tour brochures are among the materials available at the Chamber Office. Also, arrange for group tours at the Chamber.

Annual Events

March

• St. Patrick's Day Parade & Bed Races — Join in for a fun day of hilarity and excitement at downtown's annual Celtic celebration featuring the appearance of Kansas City's St. Andrew Pipes and Drums

May-September

• State Fair Motor Speedway —

Discover the thrills of dirt track racing at the only one-half mile dirt track in Missouri. Featuring three racing classes. Winged sprint cars, modifieds, and street stocks.Friday nights during the racing season. 1-800-499-RACE

June

• Scott Joplin Ragtime Festival — This festival features five days and four nights of ragtime concerts and music hall shows, symposia, tea dances, historical presentations, sheet music exchanges, ragtime contests, and a myriad of other activities — all fun, and many free!
1-800-827-5295 or
(660) 826-2271

• Bothwell Lodge Garden Party — Go back in time to the turn-of-the century as you tour Bothwell Lodge, participate in period games, and enjoy speakers and demonstrations. Bothwell Lodge State Historic Site.
(660) 827-0510

July

• Missouri State Pow-Wow — This authentic intertribal American Indian gathering features three days of native American culture food, dancing, and arts and crafts including silver jewelry, furs, pottery, and paintings.
1-800-827-5295
or (660) 826-5608

August

• Missouri State Fair —

Fairgrounds 16th and Limit Avenue. One of the country's leading state fairs. Stage shows, rodeo, competitive exhibits, livestock, auto races. (660) 530-5600.

September
- Fall Fest — This event features staged entertainment crafts and artisans.

November
- ABWA Craft Show
- Antique Show
- Show-Me Crafters Craft Show

December
- Xi Beta Upsilon Craft Show

Shopping and Dining

The city of 20,000 inhabitants is loaded with antique and craft shops, many within proximity of the downtown area. Also, an abundance of eating facilities are strategically located.

In Conclusion

For further information contact:
Sedalia Area Chamber of Commerce: 113 E. 4th
Sedalia, MO 65301
1-800-827-5295 • (660) 826-2222
FAX:(660) 826-2223
Web Site:
   http://tourism.sedalia.mo.us
E-mail: cofc@iland.net

66 From the moment you first step into our city, you'll feel the richness of our heritage. Founded in 1860, Sedalia began as a rough frontier town in the new west. Our Historic District features Missouri's first Carnegie Library, antique shops and quaint stores. You may also tour an authentic Missouri "castle," Bothwell Lodge State Historic Site. In its early years, Sedalia's economy was built on the railroad. Today, the country's largest rail to trail conversion, the Katy Trail State Park, winds through town.

The Missouri State Fairgrounds and its 396 acres of exhibit areas, 2,200 site campground and historic facilities have become one of the hallmarks of Sedalia. Besides offering one of the largest ten day fairs in America, the Fairgrounds also hosts many other events throughout the year — livestock shows, camping events, sporting events, horse and car races and truck pulls.

Come celebrate the birth of ragtime with us at the Scott Joplin Ragtime Festival or experience Native American Culture at the Missouri State Pow Wow. Whether you are coming for festivals or fairs, for history or hospitality, we always look forward to your visit. 99 *—Melody Withers,Director*
Sedalia Area Chamber of Commerce

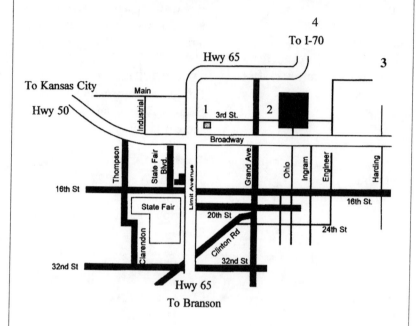

Sedalia

4
To I-70

Hwy 65

3

To Kansas City

Hwy 50

Main

Industrial

1   3rd St.   2

Broadway

Thompson

State Fair Blvd.

Limit Avenue

Grand Ave.

Ohio

Ingram

Engineer

Harding

16th St

State Fair

Clarendon

20th St

Clinton Rd

32nd St

16th St.

24th St

32nd St

Hwy 65
To Branson

1. Chamber of Commerce
2. Historical District
3. Katy Trail State Park
4. Bothwell Lodge State Historic Site

St. Charles
"Missouri's First Capitol"

Location
Located along Interstate 70 west of St. Louis.

History
The roots of St. Charles go back to the year 1769, when a French Canadian fur trader by the name of Louis Blanchette founded a small settlement he promptly called "Les Petite Cotes" (The Little Hills). In 1804 Merriwether Lewis and William Clark began their infamous expedition from the banks of the Missouri River at St. Charles. In 1816, Mother Philippine Duchesne led a group from France that established the Academy of the Sacred Heart, the first free school west of the Mississippi, in the St. Charles area.

After Missouri obtained its statehood, St. Charles was initially chosen as the capital and served as such from 1821 to 1826. Even after the capital was moved to centrally located Jefferson City, St. Charles continued to grow as hundreds of German immigrants combined their efforts with those of Kentuckians and Virginians to tame the land along the Missouri River.

Today, much of St. Charles' 18th century charm has been restored, and walking along its streets recreates those early years of its grandeur.

➮ Getting Started
Much of St. Charles' history lies along the brick sidewalks of Historic Main Street. You'll want to get your daytrip started with a stop by the Tourism Center located at 230 South Main.

Attractions

Historic Main Street District
Here, along a 14-block area, you'll find the restored shops and homes of early St. Charles open for visitors. The hanging signs with their olde-style lettering greatly enhance the atmosphere.

Cavern Springs Winery
(314) 947-1200
300 Water Street
Only two blocks from the Missouri River, this winery offers tasting and tours.

First Missouri State Capitol
(314) 946-9282
200-216 South Main Street

Complex contains restored buildings that housed the state legislature from 1821 - 1826.

Goldenrod Showboat
(314) 946-2020
1000 Riverside Drive
Matinee and evening Broadway performances highlight this year-round dinner theatre. Call for reservations.

Katy Trail
The Katy Trail is a 230 mile hiking/bicycling trail which begins in St. Charles and ends in Sedalia. The trail was developed from a former Missouri, Kansas, Texas railroad right-of-way. It is operated and maintained by the Missouri Department of Natural Resources.

Lewis and Clark Center
(314) 947-3199
701 Riverside Drive
This exposition contains dioramas and other artifacts that relate the story of the famous journey.

Shrine of St. Philippine Duchesne
(314) 946-6127
619 North 2nd Street
The first free school in the west was established in 1818.

The Haviland Platter Museum
(314) 925-0745
625 South Main Street

Unique display of Haviland China in the elegance of a Nationally Registered Historic House.

Miniature World Museum and Hall of Fame
(314) 916-0550
132-136 North Main
8,000 square feet of meticulously detailed miniature representations by world renown artists

Satellite Attractions

☙ Augusta
Located southwest along Highway 94.

Augusta Historic Community
(314) 228-4005
An 1836 town including Mount Pleasant Winery and historic homes.

Montelle Winery
(314) 228-4464
Highway 94
Situated 400 feet high on a bluff overlooking the Missouri River. The winery offers tasting and special events.

Mount Pleasant Winery
(314) 482-4419
Established in 1881 in the heart of Augusta — Features tours, tasting and picnic areas.

☙ Dutzow
Located just west of Augusta, this village is the home of

Blumenhof Winery (314) 433-2245, where you can sample some of Missouri's fine wines. It was founded in 1832 by the Berlin Emigration Society.

◉ Defiance
Located southwest along Highway 94.

Sugar Creek Winery
(314) 987-2400
Situated on the bluffs overlooking the Missouri River — tasting.

Daniel Boone Home
(314) 987-2251
Highway 94 to 1868 Highway F Ole Dan'l's homestead in Missouri. Inside the 1810 construction you'll find an array of antique furnishings; outside, you'll find the Judgment Tree.

◉ St. Peters
This adjacent community just west of St. Charles was originally a parish in 1820.

Holiday Inn Dinner Theatre
(314) 946-7755
4221 South Outer Road
Dinner and drama for reasonable price. Call for reservations.

◉ Wentzville
Founded in 1855 this old town named for a chief engineer of the St. Louis, Kansas City and Northern Railway is located just west along Interstate 70.

Wentzville Historical Society Museum
(314) 332-9821
506 South Linn Avenue
Nineteenth century local history is on display.
◯ FREE ADMISSION

Annual Events

March
- County Peddler Art Show
- Annual Antique Show of the St. Charles Historical Society

May
- Lewis and Clark Rendezvous — This is the premier event in St. Charles. Costumed re-enactors, a fife and drum corps, black powder shoots, and a host of early American crafts highlight the weekend.
- Music on Main — third Wednesday of the month May-Sept. North Main Street Park with food, drinks and music.

July
- Fourth of July Light Up the Sky —Frontier Park comes alive during this holiday event.

August
- Festival of the Little Hills — More than 300,000 people attend this popular event filled with crafts—variety of entertainment.

September
- Civil War Living History Demonstration
- Goldenrod Showboat Ragtime Festival

- The Blue and Gray entertain in costume.
- Bluegrass Festival
- Mosaics — Festival of the Arts

October
- Octoberfest — City-wide celebrations honoring the French and German traditions.
- Missouri River Story Festival —Weekend of storytelling and ghost stories.

December
- Christmas Traditions Weeks — Beginning after Thanksgiving, an assortment of holiday activities from Yule logs to candlelight shopping are on tap.

Shopping and Dining

Much of your bargain hunting and eating will take place along the Historic Main Street. There are other facilities around town, and in many cases, these satellite locations are worth the trip.

In Conclusion

For more information contact:
St. Charles Convention and Visitors Bureau
230 South Main Street
St. Charles, MO 63301
800 366-2427
Email: gsccvb
Web Site: historicstcharles.com
FAX: (314) 949-3217

Tips

✔ Some of the shops and restaurants are closed on Mondays.
✔ There's plenty of free parking along Main Street, but if you get an early enough start, you can park behind the Visitors Center.

❝ Williamsburg West" is how Southern Living Magazine describes Historic Saint Charles. It is an excellent example of the will of a few hearty souls to preserve a Slice of Americana. One does feel the souls of a past era in this Missouri River Town where romance abounds and hospitality is a way of life. Saint Charles is a place where memories are made and history comes alive everyday. The sounds of the river, the music of the fife and the clopping of horses hoofs are your invitation to return over and over to Historic Saint Charles. ❞

—Stephen Powell, Director
The Greater Saint Charles Convention
and Visitors Bureau

St. Charles

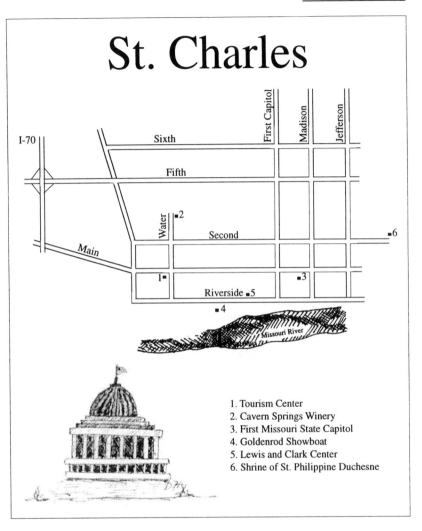

1. Tourism Center
2. Cavern Springs Winery
3. First Missouri State Capitol
4. Goldenrod Showboat
5. Lewis and Clark Center
6. Shrine of St. Philippine Duchesne

St. Louis
"Gateway to the West"

Location

Located along Interstate 70 at the easternmost border with the Mississippi River.

History

St. Louis traces its roots back to 1764 when a French village was started along the muddy banks of the Mississippi River. Following the Lewis and Clark expedition in 1804, settlers began traveling through the town on their trek out west. Many of these early trappers and explorers would return to the growing community laden with pelts and wild tales of the rugged western frontier.

Following statehood, Missouri's government was initially conducted in nearby St. Charles, but in 1826 moved westward to Jefferson City. But businesses in St. Louis retained a viable influence over the course of decisions about the future growth of the state, and though St. Louis was not the capital, it nonetheless figured prominently in the state's rise in prominence.

When the tumult of the Civil War broke, St. Louisians were divided about their loyalties. The French and Virginia/Kentucky settlers were more inclined to support the South with their common opinions on slave labor. However, St. Louis' greater number of immigrants — primarily German and Irish — were more abolitionist and adamantly supportive of Mr. Lincoln's call for union. The immigrant population, with the support of Federal troops, insured the city's control by the North.

Following the War, St. Louis looked to the new innovations in transportation to continue its growth. Bridges spanning the Mississippi enabled pedestrians, wagons, and later trains to continue their travels west. This steadily increasing number of travelers brought wealth to the area that was translated into structural and industrial growth.

Today, St. Louis continues its growth record by keeping pace with other major metropolitan cities in the United States. Industry, sports, and satisfied residents all assist in maintaining a record of excellence in this city still called the "Gateway to the West."

The St. Louis Skyline Featuring the Gateway Arch

➡ Getting Started

A good place to begin would be at the St. Louis Convention and Visitors Commission's Visitor Information Center located in America's Center on the corner of 7th and Washington. They are open 7 days a week to help you with information, brochures, and maps.

Attractions

✦ Arts and Crafts

St. Louis is home to a host of artistry and craft exhibitions with a wide variety of displays.

Craft Alliance Gallery
(314) 725-1151
6640 Delmar
Visual arts and craft exhibitions combine with educational programs.

Forum for Contemporary Art
(314) 535-4660
3540 Washington Avenue
This art museum specializes in contemporary form.

Gomes Gallery
(314) 725-1808
7513 Forsyth Blvd
Contemporary and traditional southwestern art are on display.

St. Louis Art Museum
(314) 721-0072
Forest Park
One of the focal points of the 1904 World's Fair houses a collection ranging from ancient to contemporary.

✦ Churches

There are many historical houses of worship in the St. Louis area to appreciate more than just on Sundays.

Cathedral Basilica of St. Louis
(314) 533-0544
4431 Lindell Blvd
The world's largest collection of mosaic art is contained within this spectacular church of Romanesque-Byzantine construction.

Christ Church Cathedral
(314) 231-3454
1210 Locust
The oldest Episcopal services west of the Mississippi are conducted in this 1888 English Gothic-styled church.

Old Cathedral
(314) 231-3250
209 Walnut
The oldest church in St. Louis is more than 155 years old.

✦ Education

St. Louis is home to various centers of scientific, social, and cultural education.

Big Future Inc.
(341) 256-8488

Japanese Garden at the Missouri Botanical Garden

14125 Clayton Road
This is an interactive theme house for all ages.

Missouri Botanical Garden
(314) 577-5100
4344 Shaw
Flowers, plants, trees and good scents await the visitor to this outstanding collection.

St. Louis Science Center
(314) 289-4444
5050 Oakland Avenue
More than 650 free hands-on exhibits await you at this large complex that houses a planetarium, animated dinosaurs, laser shows, and Omnimax Theater.

St. Louis Walk of Fame
(314) 727-STAR
6504 Delmar
More than 50 famous St. Louisians are honored with informative plaques and displays along the sidewalks.

St. Louis Zoo
(314) 781-0900
Forest Park
The world-class Zoo has more than 6,000 animals on 83 acres in indoor and outdoor exhibits.
✪ FREE ADMISSION

Entertainment
St. Louis is home to a vast array of contemporary entertainment.

St. Louis the Crusader

Big Cat Country at the St. Louis Zoo

The following is a list of the major centers of music, dance, and theater. Call for show information.

- **The American Theater**
  314-962-4000
- **Center of Contemporary Arts**
  314-725-6555
- **Dance St. Louis**
  314-534-5000
- **Dental Health Theater**
  314-241-7391
- **Fox Theatre**
  314-534-1678
- **Bob Kramer's Marionettes**
  314-531-3313
- **The Muny**
  314-361-1900
- **Opera Theater of St. Louis**
  314-961-0644
- **Repertory Theatre of St. Louis**
  314-968-4925
- **Riverport Amphitheater**

314-298-9944
- **Saint Louis Symphony Orchestra**
  314-534-1700
- **St. Louis Black Repertory Company**
  314-534-3810
- **Sheldon Arts Foundation**
  314-533-9900
- **Stages St. Louis**
  314-821-3322
- **Westport Playhouse**
  314-878-3322

Dinner Theaters

If dinner is what you need to perk up your appetite for drama, try one of these fabulous dinner theaters.
- **Bissell Mansion Mystery Dinner Theater**
  (314) 533-9830
- **Goldenrod Showboat Dinner Theatre**
  (314) 946-2020
- **Royal Dumpe Theater**
  (314) 621-5800

Fashions of the Past
(314) 821-0184
825 Lynda Court
Authentic clothing and accessories are modeled by men and women, and accompanied by informative narration.

Grand Center Arts and Entertainment District
314-533-1884
634 N. Grand Blvd

Here you can obtain show and ticket information on any of St. Louis' fine theaters.

Homes

St. Louis has an abundance of magnificent historical homes, many are furnished with period furniture and open for tours.

Campbell House Museum
(314) 421-0325
1508 Locust Street
This 1851 structure was home to Colonel Robert Campbell, courageous mountain man and successful fur trader.

Daniel Bissell House
(314) 868-0973
10225 Bellefontaine Road
An 1816 restored home inhabited by the general who commanded the first American military outpost west of the Mississippi.

DeMenil Mansion and Museum
(314) 771-5828
3352 DeMenil Place
This is for the architectural enthusiast interested in Greek Revival style.

Grant's Farm
(314) 843-1700
10501 Gravios
Come to Ulysses S. Grant's old homestead and enjoy a train ride with your children.

Milles Sculpture Fountain at St. Louis Union Station

✪ FREE ADMISSION
Reservations are required

Hawken House
(314) 968-1857
1155 South Rock Hill Road
The restored 1857 home is operated by the Webster Grove Historical Society.

John B. Meyers House
(314) 921-4606
180 Dunn Road

A late 1860's restored home that contains a doll and toy museum.

Sappington House Complex
(314) 957-4785
1015 South Sappington Road
Built in 1808, this structure is loaded with antiques.

Scott Joplin House
(314) 533-1003
2658 Delmar
This is the only remaining residence

associated with famous ragtime composer Scott Joplin.

Taille de Noyer
(314) 542-1100
1896 South Florissant Road
From its original log beginnings in 1790 to later nineteenth century additions, this home continues to stand.

Thornhill
(314) 532-7298
Faust County Park
Restored 1819 home of Missouri's second governor, Frederick Bates.

Municipal
The following are more general attractions in St. Louis.

Anheuser-Busch Brewery Tours
(314) 577-2626
Interstate 55 and Arsenal Street
This exhibit includes stops by the famous Clydesdale stables, as well as a many areas that demonstrate how breweries operated in earlier days.
✪ FREE ADMISSION

International Bowling Museum and Cardinal Hall of Fame
(341) 231-6340
111 Stadium Plaza
Take a tour through Cardinal history, pay homage to the great ones of the game. The Bowling Hall of Fame traces the history and evolution of the sport.

Gateway Arch
(314) 982-1410
Memorial Drive
The trademark of St. Louis is some 630 feet tall and offers a tram ride to the top from where you'll get a spectacular view. In the basement you'll find the Arch Odyssey Theater and the Museum of Westward Expansion.

Old Courthouse
(314) 425-4468
11 North 4th Street
Visit the scene of the historical Dred Scott trial.
✪ FREE ADMISSION

Union Station
(314) 421-6655
Market Street and 18th
This refurbished old train station is filled with shops and restaurants along with special activities and performances.

Museums
There's no end to the variety of expositions you'll find in the St. Louis area. There is something for everyone.

Bigfoot 4x4 Inc.
(314) 731-2822
6311 North Lindbergh Blvd
Here you will find a big trucker's delight with displays about the world's largest truck. Bigfoot fans will be in for a BIG thrill.

Laclede's Landing in St. Louis

Saint Louis Art Museum
(314) 721-0072
1 Fine Arts Drive
The Art Museum is one of the leading art museums in the country. Its history dates back to 1904 when it was constructed for the World's Fair held in Forest Park. Collections range from ancient and contemporary to Renaissance and Impressionism.

Carondelet Historic Center
(314) 481-6303

6303 Michigan Avenue
Site of first Missouri kindergarten 1873.

American Kennel Club Museum of the Dog
(314) 821-3647
1721 South Mason Road
All of the doggone history about canines that you could ever ask for is here.

Eugene Field House and St. Louis Toy Museum
(314) 421-4689
634 South Broadway
Be introduced to the well-known children's poet at his boyhood home.

Golden Eagle River Museum
(314) 846-9073
Bee Tree Park
River travel from rafts to steamboats are showcased here.
✪ FREE ADMISSION

History Museum
(314) 746-4599
Forest Park
Four levels of St. Louis history are available at the museum.
✪ FREE ADMISSION

Jefferson Barracks
(314) 544-5714
533 Grant Road
Museums depict the history of this old facility that once had the likes of Robert E. Lee and Ulysses S. Grant as its residents.

Laclede's Landing Wax Museum
(314) 241-1155
720 North 2nd Street
Over 180 wax figures from London are on display.

City Museum
(314) 231-CITY
701 N. 15th Street

City museum is a place of fantasy and wonder, mystery and craft. It is housed in three floors of a downtown landmark building. Exhibits range from caves and the world's largest windmill to a giant bowhead whale and fish tank

Museum of Western Jesuit Missions
(314) 837-3525
700 Howdershell Road
The history of early American mission work is displayed through various artifacts.

Soldiers' Memorial Museum
(314) 622-4550
1315 Chestnut
A military museum pays tribute to veterans from all wars.

Satellite Attractions

St. Louis is surrounded by several communities that offer excellent attractions.

🌿 **Eureka**
Established as a mining camp in 1853 and a town in 1858, this community is located west along Interstate 44. For further information call the Eureka Tourism Commission at (573) 938-5233.

Six Flags Over Mid-America
(314) 938-4800
Interstate 44 Exit 261

This popular theme park is open May through Labor Day seven days a week, and weekends in April and October.

Santa's Magical Kingdom
(314) 938-5925
Next to Six Flags
A seasonal November through January attraction featuring Christmas animation, and more than 2 million lights.

❦ Gray Summit
Along Interstate 44.

Purina Farms
(314) 982-3232
Interstate 44 to Highway 100 to County Road
An extravaganza of domestic animal displays await you here. Learn how to take better care of your pets.
✪ FREE ADMISSION

❦ High Ridge
Located south along State Road 30.

Poco-Loco Western Town and Museum
(314) 677-5555
6004 Antire Road
Relive the 1880's in this recreated western town complete with gun fights, shooting gallery and movies.

❦ Kimmswick
This satellite community is located along Interstate 55 at Highway K. History and antiques highlight this 1859 German settlement along the Mississippi. For further information, stop by the Kimmswick Visitor's Center at 314 Market Street, or call (314) 464-0779.

❦ Kirkwood
This western suburb of St. Louis has an assortment of activities to choose from. For further information stop by the Kirkwood Chamber of Commerce and Tourism at 138 West Madison or call (314) 821-4161.

Museum of Transportation
(314) 965-7998
3015 Barrett Station Road
Locomotives, famous cars, and even the Good Ship Lollipop are on tap here at this museum.

The Magic House Children's Museum
(314) 822-8900
516 South Kirkwood Road
A fun attractions for kids 1 to 100. A must for grandparent's.

Special Tours

Delta Queen and Mississippi Queen
(800) 543-1949
Take a riverboat cruise into adventure. The boats depart from St. Louis May through October.

Annual Events

There are many annual events in St. Louis that if they occurred in a smaller community would merit listing here. For events like special performances or exhibitions contact the Convention and Visitors Commission 1-800-916-0040 for further details. The following reflect a list of annual community events that are enjoyed by people from all over the region.

February
- Mardi Gras St. Louis — There are eleven days of gala fun in historic Soulard.

March
- St. Patrick's Day Parade and Run —The downtown becomes filled with both Irish and non-Irish.
- Mid-America Jazz Festival — If you're good, you're playing here.

May
- American Indian Pow Wow — Jefferson Barracks hosts this festival displaying Native American history and culture.
- Gypsy Caravan — More than 600 vendors make this a popular event.

July
- Fair St. Louis — Parades, rides, shows, foods, and half of Missouri can be found at this annual event on the Gateway Arch grounds.
- Soulard Bastille Day

- Explore French festivities at this event.
- Black Family Week Summerfest — Music, workshops and lectures commemorate and explore the roots of the African-American family. This takes place at Ivory Peery Memorial Park.

August
- St. Louis Strassenfest— German festivities at the Memorial plaza.

September
- Labor Day Parade — Floats and marching bands galore go through downtown St. Louis.
- St. Louis County Fair and Air Show — This three day extravaganza is at the Spirit of St. Louis Airport west on Highway 40.
- St. Louis Blues Heritage Festival — A fitting event in one of the blues capitals of the world, performances occur in various locations throughout the downtown area.
- St. Louis Art Fair — Artists from around the U.S. exhibit their talents in the Clayton Central Business District.
- Great Forest Park Balloon Race — There's more than hot air at this popular event.

October
- Apple Butter Festival — Kimmswick is the site of this gala affair.

November
- Veteran's Day Parade — Floats,

marching bands, and excitement abound in downtown St. Louis at the parade

December

- Annual Way of the Lights — Hundreds of thousands of Christmas lights showcase this event at the National Shrine of Our Lady of the Snows.
- Christmas Parade — A Christmas season celebration in downtown St. Louis is a tradition.
- First Night St. Louis — Bring in the New Year with fireworks and celebration in downtown St. Louis.

Shopping and Dining

Suffice it to say, if you have the money, the urge, and the appetite, St. Louis is just the place for you.

In Conclusion

For further information contact: St. Louis Convention and Visitors Bureau

One Metropolitan Square
Suite 1100
St. Louis, MO 63102
(800) 916-0040
Email: tourism@st-louis-cvc.com
Web Site: www.st-louis-cvc.com
Fax: 314 421 0394

Tips

✔ Forest Park contains a number of prime attractions, so it's a good destination on its own.

✔ Keep track of annual special events. Often you can save on package offers.

✔ Order a copy of the official St. Louis Visitors Guide offered by the Convention and Visitors Commission. It is free!

✔ If you plan on attending one of the major events, get there early for parking.

✔ If you don't like city driving, try the MetroLink (314) 231-2345. It will take you to most areas of interest for a modest price.

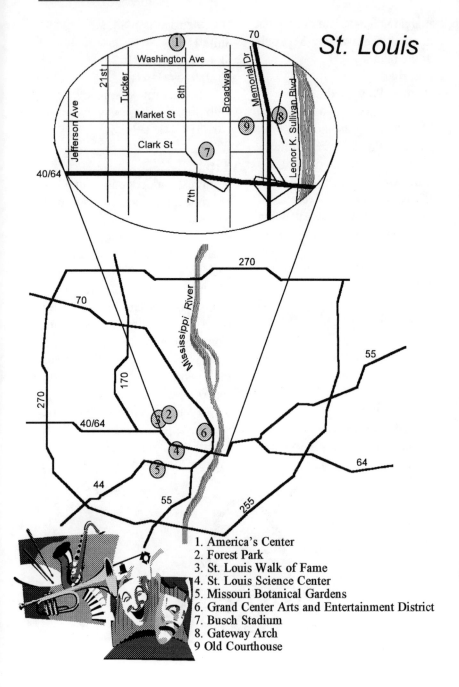

St. Louis

1. America's Center
2. Forest Park
3. St. Louis Walk of Fame
4. St. Louis Science Center
5. Missouri Botanical Gardens
6. Grand Center Arts and Entertainment District
7. Busch Stadium
8. Gateway Arch
9 Old Courthouse

❝ Venture into St. Louis and discover a lively mixture of America's colorful past, present and future. America's Center, St. Louis newly expanded convention center complex, boasts the sparkling new Trans World Dome, home of the St. Louis Rams and an additional 162,000 square feet of prime exhibit space. The entire America's Center facility includes 502,000 square feet of prime exhibit space; 80 meeting rooms; a 28,000 square foot ballroom; a 1,411 seat lecture hall; and the only Information Association of Conference Centers approved conference center within a convention in the United States.

St. Louis is proud of its history. Historical treasures include the beautifully restored Union Station, an architectural masterpiece housing shops, restaurants and cafes, and the breathtaking Grand Hall. A monument to modern times, the magnificent Gateway Arch offers a spectacular view of the city skyline and the boats plying the Mississippi River. Visit nearby Laclede's Landing, a lively center for business, dining and entertainment, or the tranquil Missouri Botanical Garden which includes a lovely 14-acre Japanese Garden. Forest Park offers 1,300 acres of placid beauty as well as the St. Louis Zoo, Art Museum, and History Museum. Plus, St. Louis is home to over 40 working blues bands, so you don't have to look too far to experience good music and good times.

One visit, and you'll see why St. Louis, once the starting point for so many journeys, is now a favorite destination for travelers from around the world. ❞

—Mary Hendron
Associate Director of Public Relations
St. Louis Convention and Visitors Commission

Warrensburg
"A Good Place to Visit, A Great Place to Live"

Location

We are located at the intersection of Highway 50 and Route 13, southeast of Kansas City, in Johnson County. When traveling down Interstate 70 exit at Route 13 and go south.

History

The community's beginnings go back to 1833 when Martin Warren, a transplant from Kentucky, came to the area and built a log cabin near the Osage Indian Trail. The town was officially incorporated in 1855.

Warrensburg is most famous for being known as an Animal Loving Community. In 1869 during a famous trial, Senator Graham Vest wrote a eulogy to Old Drum, a dog who had been shot and killed by a neighbor. From this eulogy the phrase, "A Man's Best Friend is his Dog" was coined. This trial and Old Drum has sparked animal lovers from around the world to visit Warrensburg and review the fate of Old Drum.

Warrensburg has always been known for their dedication to education. In 1919 the founding of Central State Teachers College brought higher education to Warrensburg. In 1946 the college was renamed to Central Missouri State College and then in 1972 it was again renamed as Central Missouri State University. The campus of CMSU in itself is worth visiting for a day.

➡️Getting Started

A definite first stop for you daytrip would be one of the feature attractions in Warrensburg which is the former Missouri Pacific Railroad Depot, built in 1890 and located at 100 South Holden Street. The Depot is home of the Warrensburg Chamber of Commerce and the beginning of the historic walking tour of Warrensburg.

Attractions

1897 Johnson County Courthouse
(660) 747-5288
Holden Street
A memorial for Old Drum stands on the lawn to honor mans best friend. Inside the courthouse provides historical travel back through time as items from the Centennial Cornerstone are on display.

CMSU Museum and Archives
(660) 543-4649
Clark Hall
Tour a variety of art exhibits and the beautiful art gallery which exist on the campus of Central Missouri State University.

Mary Miller Smiser
Heritage Library and Museum
(660) 747-6480
302 North Main
Memories of Johnson County are on display as you travel back through time to an 1850's Courthouse and the Old School house, which both have been restored and are open to the public to view. The museum which surrounds both structures contains a wide variety of artifacts of Johnson County and is a delight to view especially for those history buffs visiting the area.

Warrensburg Community Center
(660) 747-7178
445 E. Gay Street
This is a definite stop for those passing through Warrensburg. The brand new state of the art facility houses three indoor swimming pools, including one therapeutic pool, an indoor track, full weight room, basketball courts, arts and crafts room, and is home to the Warrensburg Senior Center.

Old Courthouse
300 North Main Street
A restored 1838 structure.

James C. Kirkpatrick Library
Located on the campus of Central Missouri State University. This state of the art facility will take education into the next century with technology and will encourage education for years to come.

Satellite Attractions

❧ **Clinton**
The seat of Henry County, organized in 1834, is located south along State Route 13.

Henry County Museum and
Cultural Arts Center
(660) 885-8414
203 West Franklin Street
This 1886 Anheuser-Busch building contains historical relics.

❧ **Concordia**
This German community was founded in 1868, and today is located north along Interstate 70.

Lohoefener House Museum
(660) 886-2629
710 Orange Street
An 1873 German home to visit.

Whiteman Air Force Base
(660) 687-6125
Nine miles east of Warrensburg Warrensburg helps host for the Whiteman Air Force Base Air Show which is held annually and open to the public. Whiteman AFB is 12 miles east of Warrensburg on Highway 50. Come visit the home of the B-2 Stealth Bomber and view

all of the planes and flying exhibits during the annual air show.

Annual Events

June

• Main Street Arts Festival — This annual event brings artist from around the state to exhibit their wide variety of artistic abilities. Call the chamber office for details and dates.

September

• Fall Festival — The Warrensburg community celebrates the fall harvest by hosting the annual Fall Festival. This three day event brings in local and professional musicians, carnival rides for the young and young at heart, a wide variety of arts and crafts vendors and especially noteworthy is the *Antique Classic Car* show which hosts over 150 vintage cars each year. This festival is a must as it has something for everyone.

• Johnson County Rodeo — This annual event is usually held in conjunction with the Fall Festival. For exact dates each year call the Chamber office.

December

• Nightime Holiday Parade — The Christmas holidays bring an added pleasure to Warrensburg as the season is celebrated with a night time parade. This annual event has developed into a parade of over 70 entries and definitely entices all of the Ebenezer Scrooges into the holiday season.

Shopping and Dining

Warrensburg offers a wide variety of shopping and dining and has an ample variety of specialty shops, antiques and dining establishments.

In Conclusion

For further information contact:
Warrensburg Chamber of
Commerce 100 S. Holden Street
Warrensburg, MO 64093
(660) 747-3168
E-mail:
wrbgchmbr@sprintmail.com
FAX: (660) 429-5490
Look for us on the World Wide Web

66 Warrensburg has the warmth and friendliness of a small town, with a population of 17,000 and an additional 12,000 when CMSU is in session, but we also offer many big city amenities, like our Community Center. Please call our office with any question you may have on our community or stop by our office for a cup of coffee and Welcome to Warrensburg Package as you travel through. 99

—*Warrensburg Chamber of Commerce*

Daytrip Missouri
Interstate 44

Branson
"America's Live Entertainment Capital"

Location
Located on Highway 65, south of Springfield, in Taney County.

History
Branson was a quiet settlement until the early 1900s when a novel entitled, "Shepherd of the Hills," was published. Written by Harold Bell Wright, the book prompted immediate interest in the Ozark area, and flooded the quiet community with curiosity seekers. Visitor camps, not hotels, housed most of the earliest tourists to Branson.

The local natural recreational activities were greatly increased in 1913 with the completion of the Ozark Beach Dam near Forsythe. This created the popular Lake Taneycomo. In the 1950s, Table Rock Dam was constructed and formed Table Rock Lake. Outdoor enthusiasts increased their visits.

The 1960s brought a new attraction to Branson — one that was to change the town beyond its wildest dreams. When Hugo and Mary Herschend opened their small attraction atop Marvel Cave and called it Silver Dollar City, little did they realize what they were giving birth to.

Next came the production of "Shepherd of the Hills," which was located on the site where Wright's novel characters originated.

With these two pillars of attractions firmly established, other acts followed. The first music act to hit the town was a troupe calling itself "The Baldknobbers." Their success in staging an Ozark country repertoire led to the infusion of additional acts. After the Baldknobbers, the Presley family built the first theater or what is now known as Highway 76 or "The Strip."

Several regionally famous acts increased the visitor numbers, but it wasn't until the Roy Clark Celebrity Theatre opened in 1983 that the town really began to command national attention.

Celebrities like BoxCar Willie, Mel Tillis and others followed. Andy Williams was the first non-country performer and he was followed by entertainers such as Tony Orlando, Wayne Newton, the Lennon Sisters, Osmonds and the list keeps going.

Today, there are scores of things to do in Branson. From music and drama to rides and outdoor recreation, you'll find more to do here than you could possibly accomplish in a single day trip.

Hop aboard the Showboat Branson Belle for a unique tour of beautiful Table Rock Lake.

➡ Getting Started

The best place to begin your Branson daytrip would be at the Branson/Lakes Area Chamber of Commerce and CVB's Welcome Center. From Highway 65, just take the Highway 248 exit and look for the signs. The Center is located adjacent to the Chamber of Commerce building. There's free parking, and inside you'll find a friendly staff armed with lots of pertinent information.

Attractions

Bonniebook
(800) 539-7437
Highway 65

Visit this favorite retreat of the famous Kewpie artist, Rose O'Neil. Creations on display.

White Water
(417) 334-7487
3505 W. Hwy. 76
Sun-sational fun on 12 spash-tacular rides for the whole family.

Shepherd of the Hills Homestead
(800) 523-7589
West Highway 76
Tours of the site made famous by author, Harold Bell Wright, through his novel *Shepherd of the Hills* are available. See Old Matt's Cabin a

registered national landmark and visit the tiny Notch Post Office, which is also described in the novel.

Stone Hill Winery
(417) 334-1897
Highway 165 at Green Mountain Drive
Tasting and fine dining are available.
✪ FREE TOURS

Branson Scenic Railway
The restored depot functions as a departure point for the Branson Scenic Railway. Passengers wishing to travel south go to Lake Taneycomo traveling through historic Hollister and on into the Northern Arkansas Ozarks. While those going north pass by the James River and the scenic Roark Creek where they cross the Roark canyon trestle and through the Reeds Spring tunnel. The Vista Dome cars have been restored allowing spectacular views of the valleys and mountains.

Silver Dollar City
(800) 952-6626
Highway 76
Crafts, rides, shows, and good food all in one of Missouri's largest theme parks. You will find 100 resident craftsmen and 50 turn-of-the-century shops.

Thrill Bubble
(417) 334-1919
West Highway 76
Big wrap-around screen and awesome sound give you a 15 minute thrill.

Ozarks Discovery IMAX Theater
(417) 335-4832
3562 Shepherd of the Hills Expressway
Six stories of screen and 22,000 watts of sound bring the Ozarks to life.

Showboat Branson Belle
(800) 227-8587
Highway 165
Take a cruise on a full-sized riverboat and be entertained with a show while having dinner.

Dixie Stampede
(800) 520-5544
Highway 76 Country Blvd
Spectacular dinner theater in the round.

Museums

Hollywood Wax Museum
(417) 337-8277
5030 W. Hwy. 76, Branson
You will find famous celebrities such as John Wayne, Marilyn Monroe, Charlie Chaplin, Elvis Presley and over 170 more "living wax" stars.

Home of the Stars
(417) 339-4536
Green Mountain Drive, Branson
View replicas of stars home that
have been furnished and decorated
by Branson entertainers. You will
find the Lennon family kitchen,
Mel Tillis' living room, Tony
Orlando's dining room, Barbara
Fairchild's bedroom and many
others who are represented with
their personal memorabilia.

Ripley's Believe It or Not!
(417) 337-5300
3326 W. Hwy. 76, Branson View
the world's largest ball of twine,
see 48,000 matchsticks that have
been turned into a replica of an
aircraft carrier. You will have to
see it to believe it.

Ralph Foster Museum
(417) 334-6411
Known as the "Smithsonian of the
Ozarks." This museum is dedicated
to the history of the Ozark region.
You will find the "Beverly
Hillbillies" truck and many other
fascinating collections.

BoxCar Willie Museum
1-800-942-4626
3454 W. Hwy 76
Dedicated to the career of BoxCar
Willie. See the cockpit of the
KC97 airplane that BoxCar flew
while in the United States Air
Force.

One of Branson's Attractions

Hank's Farm Toys and Museum
(417) 337-9222
A vast array of antique collectible
toy tractors and other farm
machinery. Find this attraction in
the Branson Heights Shopping
Center on West 67 west of Roark
Valley Road.

Entertainment
Branson is the entertainment
capital of Missouri, but there are
more than country music shows to
choose from.

Murder Mystery Mayhem
Dinner Theatre
(417) 335-4700

An evening full of suspense for the brave of heart.

Shepherd of the Hills Outdoor Theatre
(418) 554-4191
102 S. 5586 West Hwy. 76
Branson's original attraction continues in an outdoor theatre.

Recreational
Some of the attractions in Branson are just plain FUN.

Roadsters U Drive
(800) 457-HONK
Highway 76
Ever want to drive a roadster? Here's your chance.

Virtual Reality Golf
(800) 280-1111
124 E. College Street
Too cold to do the real thing? Try a computer course.

✣ Theaters Music Shows
This is the staple fare of Branson activity. If you came for one of these, you may be experiencing more than just a daytrip. These are headline shows in Branson.

Andy Williams' Moon River Theatre
(417) 334-4500 • 1-800-666-6094

The "Strip" in Branson

Baldknobbers Jamboree
(417) 334-4528
Barbara Fairchild Theater
(417) 334-6400
Bobby Vinton Blue Velvet Theatre
(417) 334-2500 • 1-800-872-6229
BoxCar Willie
Ferlin Huskey
(417) 334-8696 • 1-800-942-4626
Branson Mall Music Theatre
50's At the Hop Show
(417) 335-5300 • 1-800-434-5412
Braschler Music Show
(417) 334-4363 • 1-800-789-7001
Country Tonite Theatre
(417) 334-2422 • 1-800-468-6648
The Duttons @
Barbara Fairchild Theatre
(417) 334-6400
The Grand Palace
Featuring Dino Karsonakis
(417) 335-6866 • 1-800-884-4536
Legends Family Theatre
Hughes Brothers
(417) 336-3688 • 1-800-635-3688
Jennifer's Americana Theatre
(417) 335-8176 •
1-800-4Jennifer
Jim Stafford Theatre
(417) 335-8080 • 1-800-677-8553
VanBurch Show and
Wellford Show
(417) 337-7140
Lawrence Welk Show
(417) 337-SHOW •1-800-505-Welk
Lennon Brothers Breakfast Show
(417) 337-SHOW • 1-800-505-Welk
Mel Tillis Theatre
With Pam Tillis

(417) 335-6635
Mickey Gilley Theatre
(417) 334-3210 • 1-800-334-1936
Osmond Family Theater
(417) 336-6100
Positive Country Theatre
(417) 334-7272 • 1-800-811-6555
Presleys Jubilee
(417) 334-4874
The Promise
(417) 336-4202 • 1-800-687-4752
Remember When Theatre
(417) 335-3533 • 1-800-419-4832
Remington Theatre
(417) 336-6220 • 1-800-371-3701
76 Music Hall
(417) 335-2484
Roy Clark's Celebrity Theatre
76 Country USA Brumley Show.
Down Home Country, Mountain
Jubilee, Sunday Gospel Jubilee
(417) 334-0076
The Shoji Tabuchi Theatre
(417) 334-7469
Talk of the Town Theatre
Featuring Wayne Newton and
Tony Orlando
(417) 335-2000
Waltzing Waters Theatre
(417) 334-4144 • 1-800-276-7284
Wild West Theatre
(417) 335-2738
The Yakov Smirnoff Show
(417) 33-YAKOV • 1-800-33 -
NOKGB
Owens Theatre
Elvis and the Superstars
1-800-558-4795/417-536-2112
Anita Bryant Theatre
(417) 339-3939

One of Branson's non-musical attractions—Ripley's believe it or not

**Scherlings Cowboy Cafe
Restaurant and Showroom**
1-888-234-SHOW
**Pump Boys and Dinettes
Theatre and Broadway for
Breakfast**
(417) 336 4319

Natural Attractions

If your daytrip includes the great outdoors, then the Branson area also has something to offer.

Table Rock Lake
(417) 334-4704
Highway 165
Outdoor recreations or tour the Dewey Short Dam Visitors Center.

Ozark Caves
Missouri is known as the cave state and has over 5,000 registered caves. The average temperature of 60 degrees makes them year round attractions. Marvel Cave is one of Branson's original attractions. For a list of other caves contact the Branson/Lakes Area Chamber.

Satellite Attractions

❦ Point Lookout
Located just south along State Road 248.

Ralph Foster Museum
(417) 334-6411
College of the Ozarks campus
See this collection of art, guns, and historic relics assembled by one of the pioneers of radio. Also, visit the one-room Star School.

Special Tours

There are many sites to see in Branson and a variety of ways to see them.

Branson Scenic Railway
(800) 2-Train-2
206 East Main
See the sights and the shows and let someone else fight the traffic, or try taking a ride on a real locomotive drawn train.

Lake Queen
(417) 334-3015
280 North Lake Drive
Sternwheel riverboat tour of Table Rock Lake.

Polynesian Princess
(800) 523-7589
Long Creek Road
Sightseeing and dinner cruises on Table Rock Lake.

Ride The Ducks
(417) 334-3825
Truman Road
Make an amphibious assault on Table Rock Lake and the streets of Branson.

Sammy Lane Pirate Cruise
(417) 334-3015
280 North Lake Drive
A boat tour of Table Rock Lake.

Spirit of America
(800) 867-2459
Rock Lane Resort

Dining in Branson

Help the crew sail a 48 foot Catamaran and enjoy the sights of Table Rock Lake.

Table Rock Helicopter Tours
(417) 334-6102
3309 West Highway 76
Get a better viewing vantage of the lake and surrounding area.

Annual Events

You will find no lack of events in the Branson area. For a complete list and continual updates contact the Chamber of Commerce.

April
- Silver Dollar City Opening Day
- World-Fest at Silver Dollar City
- Kewpiesta at Bonniebrook Park

May
- Plumb Nellie Days, Hillbilly Festival and Craft Show/ Sidewalk Sale
- Great American Music Festival at Silver Dollar City
- Branson Summer Holiday begins
- Branson Remembers — A Memorial Tribute
- Polka Fest at Welk Resort Center

June
- Branson Summer Family Fun begins
- National Children's Festival — Silver Dollar City

August
- Cruisin Branson Lights
- Oldtime Fiddle Contest

September
- Autumn Celebration begins
- Fall Harvest Festival
- National Festival of Craftsman

October
- Golf Tournament — Contact Chamber

November
- Ozark Mountain Christmas begins
- Candlelight Christmas Open House
- Annual Veterans Day Parade and Ceremony

December
- New Year shows at several theatres

Shopping and Dining

Branson has almost as many places to shop and eat as it has shows. For a quick daytrip, you might want to check out one of Branson's three huge outlet malls or the unique craft shops and specialty stores.

In Conclusion

Branson/ Lakes Area Chamber of Commerce and Convention and Visitors Bureau, PO Box 1897
269 State Highway 248
Branson, MO 65615-1897
(417) 334-4136
FAX (417) 334-4139
1-800-214-3661

Tips

✔ Houseboats and other water attractions are abundant on Bull Shoals as well as Table Rock Lake. Contact the Chamber of Commerce for a list of available opportunities.

✔ For the avid golfer look no farther than Branson. You will find several 18 hole championship style courses located in the Branson area. Contact the Chamber of Commerce for more information.

✔ Driving - Highway 76 is one of the busiest in America. Keep that in mind when you're trying to get somewhere. You can "choose to cruise" or "choose not to cruise" and use one of Branson's alternate routes.

✔ Higher traffic times are just prior to and just following the shows. If you prefer not to use Hwy. 76, choose one of Branson's alternate routes to reach your destination faster.

Carthage
"City Full of Historic Treasures"

Location
Located approximately 15 miles east of Joplin in Jasper County.

History
Henry Piercey built the first house and George Hornback began the first store in the town of Carthage that became the county seat of Jasper County in 1842.

The Civil War saw many of the early structures in Carthage burned by Confederate guerrillas. But following the war, lead and zinc mining brought prosperity to nearby Joplin that spilled over into Carthage. Marble quarries begun in the 1880s ensured the city's growth.

Two women who figure prominently in Cathage's history were Belle Starr and Annie Baxter. Belle Starr was the notorious cowgirl who rode for a time with Quantrill's bushwhackers. Mrs. Baxter, on the other hand, received national acclaim by other means. In 1890 she was elected to the office of county clerk, only to be prohibited from taking office by virtue of her gender. An appeal to State Supreme Court resulted in her favor and gave momentum to the women's suffrage movement.

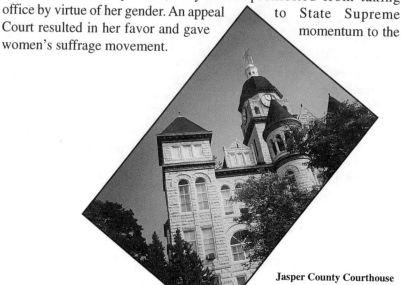

Jasper County Courthouse

➠ Getting Started

You can begin your trip with a visit to the Carthage Chamber of Commerce located at 107 East 3rd Street. This will place you close to the historic district.

Attractions

Civil War Museum
(417) 358-2667
205 East Grant
Civil War historical artifacts and a 7' by 15' mural relate the saga of the Battle of Carthage.
✪ FREE ADMISSION

Kendrick Place
(417) 358-0636
Intersection of Highways 571 and V
The 1841 restored home of William Kedrick was originally built by Sinnet Rankin. The home was witness to much of the activity surrounding the Second Battle of Carthage in 1863.

Old Cabin Shop
(417) 358-6720
West Mound Street Road
An 1838 cabin houses antique guns and Indian artifacts.

Phelps House
(417) 358-1776
1146 South Grand Ave
An historic home is open for tours.

Powers Museum
(417) 358-2667
1617 West Oak Street
An extravagant collection of the Powers family of Carthage. This exhibit contains everything from Civil War artifacts and medical instruments, to fashion collections and quilts.
✪ FREE ADMISSION

Precious Moments Chapel
(800) 543-7975
From US 71, take Fir Road (Highway HH) west, then left on Chapel Road. Nearly everyone is familiar with the tiny figurines of children with the teardrop eyes. This exhibit attracts visitors from around the country. Here you can tour the workshop studio for these famous pieces of art. In 1978 Samuel J. Butcher created these legendary art forms. In concert with sculptor Yasuhei Fujioka, Butcher gave us the Precious Moments we now find in gift shops around the world. The chapel, which was constructed in 1985, is a living memorial dedicated by Mr. Butcher to those who appreciate his art form. Its walls are covered with murals of brilliant colors depicting religious aspects of the artist's faith and inspiration. Following a guided tour, you can spend additional hours in the visitor's center that contains a restaurant, a gift shop and on the grounds you will find

—photo credit Precious Moments Chapel

Fountain of Angels at Precious Moments

an RV park, hotel, the Fountain of Angles and Precious Moments Wedding Island.

○ FREE ADMISSION

Red Oak II
(417) 358-9018
Highway 96 to Road 12
This Belle Starr museum along with a blacksmith shop, general store, and country school house recreate life on the frontier.

Special Tours

Victorian House Tour
You can take a self-guided driving tour around the streets of Carthage and enjoy its magni-ficent, well-preserved Victorian homes. A pamphlet from the Chamber of Commerce will give you a detailed account of each house on the tour.

Annual Events
July
• Precious Moment's Week — Missouri Highlights of this week-long event include signings by the artist, Samuel J. Butcher, along with special tours and craft demonstrations.

October
• Mapleleaf Festival — Enjoy a weekend filled with parades, exhibits, games, music, and food galore.

December
- Way of Salvation Lighting — This event begins the day after Thanksgiving and runs through January 1.
- Precious Moments Walk Through Christmas — A popular event at the Chapel that begins the second week in November.

Shopping and Dining

Carthage has more than an adequate number of shops and restaurants. You'll find many places to eat along Garrison and Central Avenues.

In Conclusion

For further information contact:
Carthage Chamber of Commerce
107 East 3rd
Carthage, MO 64836
(417) 358-2373
Web Site: 222.carthagenow.com
E-mail: cchamber@carthage.now
FAX: (417) 358-7479

66 For years Carthage, Missouri was known as the "Crossroads of America" for it was here, at the intersection of Central and Garrison Streets, U.S. 71 Highway and U.S. 66 finally met.

A diversity of industries and outstanding tourism attractions contribute to the healthy economic climate of this Southwest Missouri community. Among the attractions are the Precious Moments Chapel and Complex, Red Oak II, the Kendrick House, the Powers Museum, the century old Jasper County Courthouse, Victorian Homes, a delightful downtown public Square and most recently, a genuine London double-decker bus purchased by the city.

This information is meant to tantalize the reader's appetite for second helpings which can be experienced by visiting the home of "The Maple Leaf Festival" — an October event that is now 30 years old. 99

—Heather Kelly
Director
Carthage Chamber of Commerce

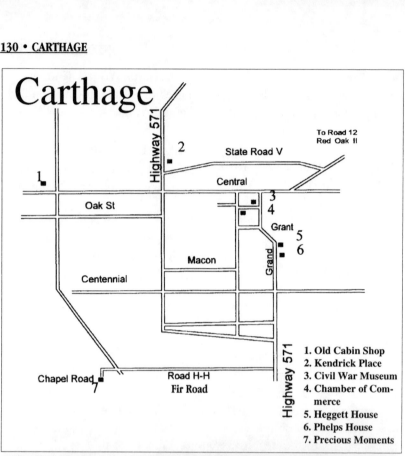

Carthage

Highway 571

2

State Road V

To Road 12
Red Oak II

1

Central

Oak St

3
4

Grant
5
6

Grand

Macon

Centennial

Highway 571

Chapel Road
7

Road H-H
Fir Road

1. Old Cabin Shop
2. Kendrick Place
3. Civil War Museum
4. Chamber of Commerce
5. Heggett House
6. Phelps House
7. Precious Moments

Civil War Reenactors in Carthage

Joplin
"Mother Lode of the Ozarks"

Location

Located at the intersection of Interstate 44 and Highway 71 in Jasper County.

History

Joplin's history begins with the settling of John C. Cox and his family from Tennessee in 1838. A store and post office were the beginnings of the town originally called Blytheville. The southwestern town rose to prominence in 1870 when a $64,000 lead strike was made. The town's name was changed to Joplin City for the Rev. Harris G. Joplin. Another early name associated with the boom town was Patrick Murphy, an Irishman who opened a miners' supply store in an adjacent town named Murphysburg. Rivalry and discord resulted in a lasting solution in 1873

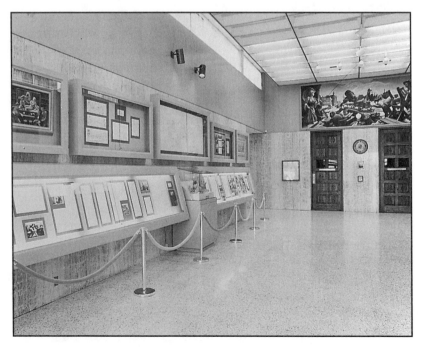

Thomas Hart Benton Mural in Joplin

when the two towns were united and incorporated into the city of Joplin. At one time this southwestern Missouri city was considered the tenth largest mining town in the world.

➡ Getting Started

Start your trip at one of the following facilities: The Joplin Area Visitor Center, which is located west of Joplin on Interstate 44, or the Joplin Convention and Visitors Bureau located at 222 West 3rd Street, inside the Georgia A. Spiva Center for the Arts.

Joplin Today

At any time of the year there is activity in Joplin and in every direction surrounding it. Boasting an abundance of hotels and restaurants, Joplin truly serves as "Host to the Four States," whether you are here for a leisurely vacation, an art exhibit, a shopping spree, or a historical tour or looking for antiques and collectibles, you are certain to enjoy your visit.

Attractions

Dorothea B. Hoover Historical Museum
(417) 623-1180
Schifferdecker Park
Dorothea B. Hoover was a local historian and preservationist in Joplin. The museum is divided into a series of rooms, each with an historical theme, and complete with mementos of Joplin's early years. Included are a doll collection, antiques, and even circus memorabilia.
✪ FREE ADMISSION

George A. Spiva Center for the Arts
(417) 623-0183
222 West 3rd
Art exhibits, workshops and tours are offered in this downtown center. Special events occur frequently throughout the year.
✪ FREE ADMISSION

Post Memorial Reference Library
300 Main Street
An artist's gold mine of information and displays on art from paintings to 16th century furniture is located inside the Joplin Public Library.

Thomas Hart Benton Permanent Exhibit
(417) 624-0820
Joplin Municipal Building
303 East 3rd Street
The 5' by 14' mural entitled "Joplin at Work at the Turn of the Century" by the famous artist Thomas Hart Benton is displayed here.
✪ FREE ADMISSION

Dorothy B. Hoover Museum

Tri-State Mineral Museum
(417) 623-2341
West 7th Street at
Schifferdecker Park
Established in 1930, the museum
depicts the zinc-lead mining
history and industry within Joplin.
Mineral samples and colorful
displays are abundant.
✪ FREE ADMISSION

Special Tours

You'll discover the Joplin area
even more personally by taking
one of their walking and or driving
tours. Check with the Bureau for
further details.

Satellite Attractions

◉ **Neosho**
The town where Governor
Claiborne Jackson and the pro-
Southern members of the Missouri
legislature met after being ousted
from Jefferson City. Neosho is
located about 15 miles south of
Joplin along Highway 71.

*Newton County Historical
Society Museum*
(417) 451-4940
Corner of Washington and
McCord Streets
More than 100 years old, this restored
jail houses an exhibit of Newton
County's history along with the Bess

Boyden Genealogy Library.

❂ FREE ADMISSION

☙ Diamond

The boyhood home of George Washington Carver was once known as Diamond Grove. It is located south along Highway Alternate 71.

George Washington Carver National Monument
(417) 325-4151
South along Highway Alternate 71
This state park honors the birthplace and achievements of the famous African-American, George Washington Carver. Born into slavery in the early 1860's on the Moses Carver Farm, young Carver spent his early years studying the mysteries of the world around him. His neighbors called him the "Plant Doctor," and later in life the determined pioneering black scientist would exercise his gifts in the realms of botany, chemistry, and agronomy. His accomplishments are preserved in photos and statues amid the surroundings of the park.

☙ Sarcoxie

Located west along Interstate 44.

Gene Taylor Library and Museum
Exits 26 and 29 on Interstate 44
Located about 25 miles east of Joplin, the museum and library are open to the public.

Annual Events

March
* American Heirloom Craft Show — This week-long popular event in Joplin also takes place again in November.

June
* Junior Ranger Program — Administered by the National Park Service, this event, which runs through the end of July, exposes children to the life of George Washington Carver as well as to their natural environment. There is no charge to this program held at the George Washington Carver National Park.

September
* Antique Show and Sale — Sponsored by the Joplin Historical Society, the proceeds of this popular event go to the Dorothea B. Hoover Museum.

October
* Applebutter Making Days — The nearby town of Mt. Vernon comes alive with this annual event.

Shopping and Dining

Joplin and its surrounding area have much to offer in the realm of antique and curio shopping. Also, Joplin's North Park Mall, with over 100 stores, is the Shopping Center for the heart of the 4 states.

Dining will be available near just about every attraction you visit.

In Conclusion

For further information contact:
Joplin Convention and
Visitors Bureau
PO Box 1384
Joplin, MO 64801
(800) 657-2534
WebSite: www.joplincvb.com

Tips

✔ There are several scenic trails in the area that the locals enjoy hiking in good weather.

✔ A popular experience is the so called, "Spook Light." If you're interested in observing a strange and mysterious sight, make a point to visit "Spookville." Located nearly 11 miles southwest near the village of Hornet you'll see an eerie light appear in the middle of a lonely road most nights. The origin of the light is unknown. Get actual directions from the Joplin Visitors Bureau.

❝ A colorful past and a lively present characterize Joplin. Rich in history, Joplin's notoriety in the late 19th and 20th century was the result of lead and zinc mining that made this bustling midwestern town one of the 10 largest mining cities in the world during its heyday.

Fascinating exhibits and information about Joplin's early days can be found at various touring attractions in our fine city.

Antiques, crafts, flea markets and other specialty shopping provide a unique appeal for visiting collectors.

Joplin also has over 1600 motel rooms to guarantee first rate services to our guests who may find more than a daytrip's worth of activities to enjoy our lovely city. ❞

—Terry Triplett, Director
Joplin Convention and Visitors Bureau

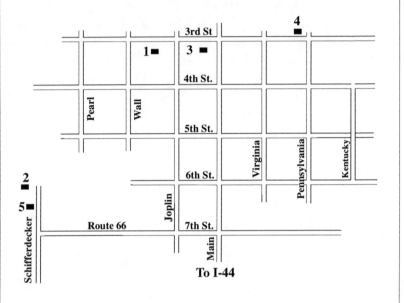

Joplin

1. Joplin Convention Center and Visitors Bureau
   . . . George A. Spiva Center for the Arts
2. Dorothea Hoover Historical Museum
3. Post Memorial Art Reference Library
4. Thomas Hart Benton Permanent Exhibit
5. Tri State Mineral Museum

Lebanon
"Crossroads of the Ozarks"

Location

Located along Interstate 44 in Laclede County.

History

According to records, Jesse Ballew settled the area in 1820 in what became known as Wyota, the name of an early Indian tribe inhabiting the area. In 1849 the renamed town of Lebanon became the county seat for Laclede County.

Visitors venturing forth to enjoy the natural attractions of the area are nothing new. As far back as the 1890s, vacationers have visited the clear-flowing water of the spring branch and Niangua River.

➡ Getting Started

You can begin your visit by stopping by the Lebanon Area Chamber of Commerce at 500 East Elm located in the new Cowan Civic Center.

With nature the headliner in Lebanon, you'll find many resorts offering group activities and family-oriented programs. The list includes:

- **Fort Niangua River Resort**
  (417) 532-4377
- **Sand Spring Resort**
  (417) 532-5857

Attractions

Bennett Springs State Park
(417) 532-4338
West along Highway 64
Missouri's third largest spring is home to fishing, hiking, dining, and camping.

I-44 Raceway
A 3/4 mile paved NASCAR sanctioned race way. Open April through September.

Annual Events

- **May**
  Annual Bennett Springs Fly Fishing Conclave
- **June**
  Bennett Springs Hillbilly Days
- **July**
  Laclede Country Fair
- **September**
  Lebanon Farm Fest
- **November**
  Holiday Festival Parade
  Christmas Pageant

In Conclusion

For further information contact:
Lebanon Area Chamber
of Commerce
321 South Jefferson
Lebanon, MO 65536
(417) 588-3256
Web Site: www.llion.org

Nevada
"Bushwhacker Capital of the World"

Location
Located on Highways 54 and 71 in Vernon County.

History
Nevada's history was earmarked by violence in the years preceding and during the Civil War, as Jayhawkers from Kansas and Confederate partisans, who were later called Bushwhackers, clashed in and around this Missouri frontier town. At one time Nevada was known as the "Bushwhacker Capital." One of the famous Bushwhacker's from Nevada was a cowboy by the name of Frank James.

➥ Getting Started
Your visit should start at the Nevada/Vernon County Chamber of Commerce located at 110 South Adams.

Attractions

Bushwhacker Museum
(417) 667-9602
212 West Walnut
Located on the corner of the courthouse square, the Moss Building (1920) housed a Ford dealership and garage.

The new home of the Nevada Public Library, its lower level houses the Bushwhacker Museum exhibits, including a replica of the Dr. J.T. Hornback house.

The Old Jail
(417) 667-5841
231 North Main
Completed in its present form in 1871, the native sandstone building served as a jail until 1960. Authentically restored in 1998.

W.F. Norman Corporation
220 North Cedar
Founded in 1898, this company is the only manufacturer of metal ceilings, made from the original dies and patterns in its 1909 catalog. A "museum in operation."
○Tours are available upon request

Bushwhacker Lake Conservation Area
Highway 43
This 3,223 facility containing a 175 acre lake offers hiking, fishing, and camping among much of Missouri's wildlife.

Radio Springs Park

Radio Springs Park
(417) 448-2742
A popular resort in the late 1800's.
Water from the well and springs
was drunk for its supposed health-
giving qualities.

Satellite Attractions

🐾 Butler
Named for William O. Butler, an
officer in the Mexican American War
in 1854, this seat for Bates County
lies north along Highway 71.

Pioneer Cabin
(816) 679-4777
100 East Fort Scott Road
Log cabin and pioneer print shop.

🐾 El Dorado Springs
Located east along Hwy 54.

Carl's Gun Shop and Museum
(417) 876-4167
100 North Main

Over 1400 guns, Missouri's largest
private display, are featured along
with unique animal mounts and
historical gun exhibits. Tours
welcome.
✪ FREE ADMISSION

Wayside Inn Museum
(417) 876-5118
119 West Spring Street
19th century hotel filled with history.

🐾 Stockton
Located east along Highway 54
to State Road 39.

Stockton State Park
(417) 276-4259
Highway 215 near Stockton
Enjoy yourself on a 2,000 acre lake.

Special Tours
The Nevada Victorian Driving
Tour offers several historic homes
and landmarks with brochures and
audio tapes to enhance the route.

Annual Events
March
- Home and Leisure Show

June
- IRPA-ACRA Sanction Professional Rodeo
- Bushwhacker Days — A weekend that features live entertainment, quilt and craft shows, a street fair and square dancing.

July
- Vernon County Youth Fair

August
- Old Settlers' Picnic — A three day celebration in Sheldon
- Clear Creek All Indian Pow Wow
- Historic East End Block Party

September
- Schell City Fall Festival
- Walker Fun Days

- Bronaugh Fall Festival

October
- Oktoberfest
- Cocklebur Days
- Missouri Osage Territory Muzzle Loaders Rendezvous

December
- Downtown Parade and MusicFest

Shopping and Dining
You'll find many shopping and eating facilities in close proximity to the downtown historic district.

In Conclusion
For further information contact:
Nevada/Vernon County Chamber of Commerce
110 South Adams
Nevada, MO 64772
1-800-910-4276
FAX (417) 667-2157

66 Nestled among the gently rolling hills in the Prairie Lands of Southwest Missouri, Nevada offers opportunities to journey into the past, become reacquainted with nature and enjoy the delights of hometown entertainment.

Your journey begins with a visit to the Bushwhacker Museum and jail, where for 100 years, this well built stone building served as the Vernon County Jail. Try our self-guided driving tour and be sure to visit the earliest known Osage Indian Village in Western Missouri. There you'll enjoy the panoramic views of the surrounding countryside and the abundant wildflowers.

When you are ready for some evening entertainment, check out the performance schedule at the Haidee and Allen Wild Center for the Performing Arts or the Community Theatre Group at the Little Alley Theatre. 99

—Kathi Wysong, Executive Director
Nevada/Vernon County Chamber of Commerce

Rolla
"A Site to Survey"

Location

Located at the junction of Interstate 44 and U.S. 63 in Phelps County.

History

In 1855, a warehouse and office were constructed in what was to become Rolla by workers building the St. Louis - San Francisco Railway. When Phelps County was organized in 1857, the tiny settlement of rail contractors had grown sufficiently to become its county seat. The town got its name from George Colledge, who, thinking of his North Carolina home, wanted to name the community after Raleigh. However, by virtue of its pronunciation, the spelling became Rolla.

The southwest branch of the Pacific Railroad was well in place by 1861. The rails around the town saw thousands of Union troops being transported to the front line during the Civil War. This boom to merchants greatly increased the town's population.

Following the war, the local economy became somewhat recessed until 1871, when the Missouri School of Mines was opened in Rolla. The facility later became the engineering school of the University of Missouri.

► Getting Started

Exploring Rolla's past is a self-guided endeavor. You can get guidance at the Rolla Chamber of Commerce building located at 1301 Kingshighway.

Attractions

Old town Rolla was located along Main Street near the Courthouse. This is the area where you will discover much of Rolla's past.

Fort Wyman
Highway 63
Remains of a Civil War fort, built in 1861 by Union forces after the battle of Wilson's Creek, can be seen.

Memoryville, USA
(573) 364-1810
Interstate 44 and Highway 63
Antique cars, art gallery and other antiques can be enjoyed.

Mineral Museum
UMR Norwood Hall

Stonehenge

The story of mineralogy is exhibited at this University facility.

Old Phelps County Jail
(573) 341-4874
3rd and Park Streets
Built in 1860, this facility used to house prisoners during the Civil War.
✪ FREE ADMISSION

Phelps County Museum
(573) 341-4874

Across from the county courthouse this two-storied log cabin contains an assortment of historical memorabilia.
✪ FREE ADMISSION

Route 66 Motors
(573) 265-5200
A living tribute to the well known Route 66 saga.

Schuman Park
Early as well as later history of railroading in America featured here.

**University of Missouri
Rolla Stonehenge**
14th and Bishop Aves
This is a partial replica of the real
thing in England.
◯ FREE ADMISSION

Satellite Attractions

◖ Fort Leonard Wood
Located west along Interstate
44.

U. S. Army Engineer Museum
(573) 341-5039
On the Army base on S. Dakota
Explore several displays and
artifacts of military engineering and
early Missouri survey techniques at
this facility.
◯ FREE ADMISSION

◖ Vienna
Located north along Highway
63.

Old Jail Museum
(573) 442-3165
Highway 63 and 42
An 1855 jail museum to tour.

◖ Waynesville
Located west along Interstate 44.

Old Stagecoach Stop
(573) 435-6766
Here you will find an 1860's
stage coach stop and Civil War
hospital.

Special Tours

Historic Rolla
This self-guided tour will take
you to many of the surviving
structures of early Rolla including:
Presbyterian Church of 1868,
Chamberlain House of 1862,
Catholic Church of 1861, Jail
house of 1860, Phelps County
Courthouse of 1860, and many
other historical sites.

Annual Events

March
• St. Patrick's Day Parade
July
• Route 66 Summerfest — The
whole town gets involved in
this festival of games,
entertainment, good food and
children's activities.
• Lions Club Carnival
August
• South Central Missouri Fair
October
• Oktorberfest
• Rolla Downtown Arts and
Crafts Festival
• This is a popular annual event
for art and craft lovers.
December
• Annual Christmas Parade

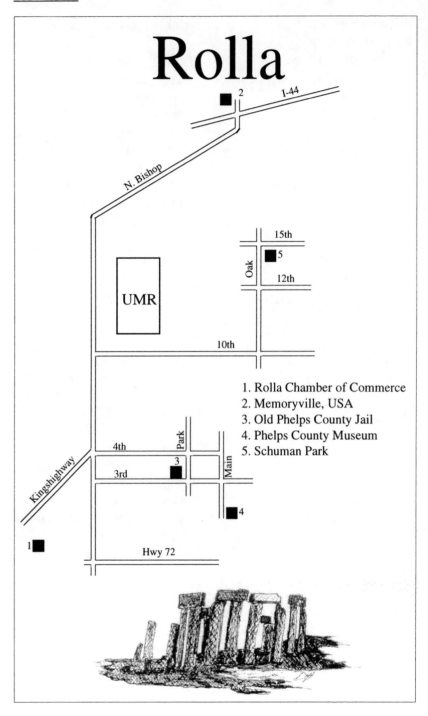

Rolla

2 I-44

N. Bishop

UMR

15th

Oak

5

12th

10th

1. Rolla Chamber of Commerce
2. Memoryville, USA
3. Old Phelps County Jail
4. Phelps County Museum
5. Schuman Park

Park

4th

3rd

3

Main

4

Kingshighway

1

Hwy 72

Shopping and Dining

With more than 600 stores reportedly in Rolla, surely you will find more than a few to your liking. For dining, expect everything from Ozark homestyle cooking to fast-food.

In Conclusion

For further information contact:
Rolla Chamber of Commerce and
Tourist Center, PO Box 823
Rolla, MO 65402
(573) 364-3577
WebSite: www.rolla.cc.com

---

66 Rolla is ranked as one of the top 100 best small towns in the U. S. And it is ranked number one in Missouri according to Norm Crampton, author of "100 Best Small Towns in America." Located in the foothills of the Ozarks at an elevation of 1,140 feet we are the "Middle of Everywhere." You can explore until your heart is content from sights along historic Route 66, wander wooded paths, fish an Ozark River, dine at our fine restaurants or stay in our clean motels. You can shop our diverse shopping atmosphere, featuring collectable antiques, interesting craft stores and hometown service from local stores. **99**

—Don Johnson
President/CEO Rolla Chamber of Commerce

Springfield
"Ozark Mountain Country's Big City"

Location
Located along Interstate 44 in Greene County, just 35 miles north of Branson.

History
The initial settling of Greene County took place in 1821 when Thomas Patterson and John Pettijohn brought their families to the area. The following year, more than 500 Delaware Indians claimed that the whole of southwest Missouri was given to them as a reservation. This event curtailed further settlements until 1830. By that time the region, called Kickapoo Prairie, began to receive another slow influx of westward traveling Americans.

In 1833 Springfield was organized by John Polk Campbell. Tradition has it that Springfield got its name from Campbell who supposedly was inspired by a field on a nearby hill with a spring on it.

Springfield was incorporated in 1838 and received its charter in 1847. By 1859 the population was about 2,500, with most employed in some form of livestock trade.

At the outbreak of the Civil War, the small town cast its lot in with the South. Both sides sought to gain control of the area early on. This culminated in the Battle of Wilson's Creek which was fought on August 10, 1861. Though Southern forces were victorious, the cost was in the life of General Nathaniel Lyon. Confederate forces would hold Springfield until 1862, when Union forces retook the town.

One of the early figures of history in Springfield was a young man by the name of Bill Hickock, who would later obtain the nickname of "Wild Bill." A dispute with another man resulted in the first public shootout in 1865, with Hickock the victor. The next year would see Wild Bill in Kansas appointed as a US Marshall.

In 1870 the Atlantic and Pacific Railroad came through the area, but chose a site a few miles north of town. Land speculators intervened, and after much wheeling and dealing, the city of North Springfield was born. By 1887, the two were consolidated into one entity. The railroad ensured the city's growth and prominence in the state.

Springfield Skyline

➼ Getting Started

You can begin your tour by stopping at the Convention and Visitors Bureau and Tourist Information Center at 3315 East Battlefield. Just get onto Highway 65 South, get off at the East Battlefield exit, and follow the signs.

Attractions

Air and Military Museum
(417) 864-7997
2305 E. Kearney Street
History of aviation and all eras of U.S. military. Memorabilia and equipment displays.

Bass Pro Shops Outdoor World
(417) 887-7334
1935 South Campbell Avenue
Seldom is a commercial establishment the big draw in the world of tourism, but this facility is a distinct exception to the rule. You don't have to be an avid fisherman or hunter to enjoy this facility. From rare aquatic life in their 140,000-gallon aquarium to awesome displays of fish and wildlife mounts, the Bass Pro Shop will lure you to more than a catch.

Dickerson Park Zoo
(417) 864-1800
3043 N. Fort Avenue
An up-close adventure with hundreds of wild animals in natural surroundings. The zoo is nationally known for its breeding of elephants, cheetahs and bald eagles.

Discovery Center
(417) 862-9910
438 St. Louis Street
An interactive, hands-on museum for children (and adults).

Fantastic Caverns
(417) 833-2010
1-44 & Highway 13 N
Ride instead of walk through the twists and turns of rock formations.
✪ 50-minute guided tour.

Bass Pro Shops Waterfall

Frisco Railroad Museum
(417) 866-7573
543 East Commercial Street
Over 2,000 items tell the story of the Frisco Railroad, one of America's early rail lines.

Gray/Campbell Farmstead
(417) 862-6293
2400 South Scenic Avenue
Oldest house in Springfield, circa 1856. Costumed guides present history of farmstead and answer questions.
✪ FREE ADMISSION

History Museum for Springfield-Greene County
(417) 864-1976
830 Boonville Avenue
Historical exhibits displayed in this 1894 City Hall. Over 30,000 books and documents and 7,000 historical photographs. Hands-on and permanent exhibits.

Japanese Stroll Garden
(417) 864-1049
2400 S. Scenic Avenue
Seven and one half acre stroll garden with extensive landscaping, including three small lakes.

Bass Pro Shops Outdoor World

Structures include a tea house, moon bridge and other unique Japanese features. Special events and festivals are held periodically.

Missouri Sports Hall of Fame
1-800-498-5678
5051 Highland Springs Blvd.
Fun-packed museum full of interactive displays and sports memorabilia.

SMSU Summer Tent Theater
417-836-5979
Enjoy summer play productions in a "Big Tent" atmosphere.

Springfield Art Museum
(417) 837-5700
1111 East Brookside Dr
Rotating year-round exhibits: Watercolor U.S.A. (June-August), a competitive exhibition of paintings from artists across the U.S. is held here
❖ FREE ADMISSION

Springfield Conservation Nature Center
(417) 888-4237
4600 S. Chrisman Avenue
Eight acres of hilly wilderness and three miles of wood chipped and

paved hiking trails with suspension bridges. Features a variety of educational exhibits, seminars, films, guided tours and special programs.

Satellite Attractions

🌾 Ash Grove

Settled and named by Colonel Nathan Boone, Daniel's youngest son, this town is located northwest along Highway 160.

Nathan Boone Homestead
Highway 160
(800) 334-6946
The restored log home belonged to one of Daniel Boone's sons.

🌾 Bolivar

North along State Road 113 to State Road 83.

North Ward Museum
(417) 326-6850
Main and Locust
Visit four buildings filled with history.

🌾 Mansfield

Located 50 miles east of Springfield, just off Highway 60.

Laura Ingalls Wilder Museum and Home
Visit the home where the Little House books were written. Museum contains artifacts, family photographs, Laura's handwritten manuscripts, Pa's fiddle and other family items.
✪ Book shop and gift store.

🌾 Republic

Located west along Highway 60.

General Sweeny's
(417) 732-1224
Highway ZZ
This Civil War museum is just north of the Wilson's Creek Battlefield.

Wilson's Creek National Battlefield
(417) 732-2662
Highway ZZ
Located just 10 miles southwest of Springfield, this National Park is the site of Missouri's first battle of the Civil War. A visitor's center and self-guided driving tour await you. During the summer months, re-enactment groups frequent the park.

🌾 Strafford

Located east along Interstate 44.

Exotic Animal Paradise
(417) 859-2016
On Route 1, along Interstate 44. More than 3,000 wild animals and rare birds roam free in their natural habitat. Tour this facility from the comfort of you own car.

Annual Events
March
- World's Fishing Fair — This popular spring show is at the Bass Pro Shop.
April
- Frisco Days — Commercial Street. 6-block long historic festival.
May
- ArtsFest — Visual and performing art festival on Historic Walnut Street.
June
- Firefall — Always held last Saturday before July 4. Springfield/Branson Regional Airport. Extravagant fireworks display with choreographed music by Springfield Symphony.
July
- Ozark Empire Fair —Missouri's second-largest fair and one of the top-rated fairs in the country.
August
- Nike Ozarks Open — Highland Springs Country Club. Professional golfers compete for a cash purse of $225,000.
September
- 1860 Lifestyle Exposition — Gray/Campbell Farmstead. Recapture a part of the past. Music, crafts, food, dancing and children's activities.
- Balloonfest — Over 40 colorful hot air balloons grace the Ozarks in a hare-and-hound race to the finish.
October
- Halloween Spooktacular — Dickerson Park Zoo. Hundreds of hand-carved jack-o'-lanterns, attractions and treats for children.
November-December
- Ozark Mountain Christmas — Over 400 lighted displays. Ongoing event also features "Festival of Lights."

Shopping and Dining
You've got loads of places for shopping and good eating to explore in the Springfield vicinity.

In Conclusion
For further information contact: Springfield Convention and Visitors Bureau
3315 E. Battlefield
Springfield, MO 65804-4048
(800) 678-8767
Call for a free Area Visitor Guide and discount coupon book.
Web Site:
   http://www.springfieldmo.org
FAX (417) 881-2231

Tips
✔ Lots of free parking.
✔ Most bus tours come in the spring and fall.

66 Surrounded by gentle mountains, green forests, deep blue lakes and clear streams of the Ozarks sits Missouri's third-largest city — Springfield!

The Ozarks only large metropolitan area, Springfield offers the best of both worlds to visitors — over 5,000 hotel rooms, more than 400 restaurants, major league shopping; and all with down home hospitality.

Experience such attractions as Bass Pro Shops Outdoors World — Missouri's #1 attraction, Exotic Animal Paradise, and Dickerson Park Zoo. Go back in time at Fantastic Caverns, Wilson's Creek National Battlefield, or General Sweeny's Civil War Museum. Stroll through one of Missouri's largest shopping centers — Battlefield Mall, or treasure hunt at our many antique shops and flea markets. Step out for a day of golf on one of our fine golf courses or head south thirty minutes for a fun day in Branson.

A trip to Springfield offers so much to see and do . . . *Ozark Mountain Country's Big City.* 99

—*Becky Hamm*
Director of Communications
Springfield Convention & Visitors Bureau

SPRINGFIELD
M I S S O U R I

Convention & Visitors Bureau
3315 East Battlefield Road, Springfield, MO 65804-4048
(417) 881-5300

Springfield

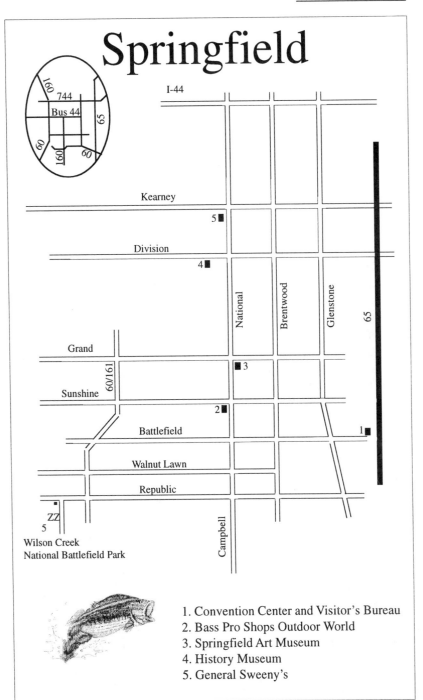

160
744
Bus 44
65
60
160
60

I-44

Kearney

5

Division

4

National

Brentwood

Glenstone

65

Grand

60/161

3

Sunshine

2

Battlefield

1

Walnut Lawn

Republic

ZZ
5

Wilson Creek
National Battlefield Park

Campbell

1. Convention Center and Visitor's Bureau
2. Bass Pro Shops Outdoor World
3. Springfield Art Museum
4. History Museum
5. General Sweeny's

St. James
"Forest City of the Ozarks"

Location
Located along Interstate 44 in Phelps County.

History
The area was first settled in 1826 when Thomas James, an Ohio banker, funded his business partner, Samuel Massey, to visit the area and explore for minerals. Finding an abundance of iron ore, Massey then established the Meramec Iron Works at the site of Meramec Spring. Land was purchased along a prairie nearby to start a settlement initially called Jamestown. However, duplicate names in the postal system necessitated a name change to Saint James.

Thomas James' son, William, immigrated to the area in 1843 and managed the Works until its closure in 1876.

In the early years, the iron was shipped by river and used in cooking utensils and farming implements. Later, as the railroads came to town, St. James continued to grow along with the demand for iron ore. By 1876, however, the furnaces began to slow in production and closed shortly thereafter.

➡ Getting Started
A good place to begin is at the Tourist Information Center located north along Highway 68 after you exit Interstate 44.

Attractions

Meramec Springs Park
(573) 265-7124
South along Highway 8
The remains of an old iron works, agriculture museum and outdoor activities await. Remains of the 1857 cold-blast furnace are still standing. A natural spring and two museums are located at the park.

Wineries
You can enjoy one of the six wineries in the St. James area. The list includes St. James, Ferrigno, Heinrichaus, Rosati, the Abby, and Peaceful Bend.

Annual Events

April
• Wine Country Bicycle Tour
JUNE
• Wine Festival
September
• Fall Wine Expo
• Grape Fall Festival
October
• Old Iron Works Days
December
• Christmas City of the Ozarks
• Parlor Tour

Shopping and Dining

You'll find an assortment of places to shop, especially along West Springfield and North Jefferson Streets. Eating facilities are dispersed throughout.

In Conclusion

For more information contact:
St. James Tourist Information Center
100 B Highway
e-mail: tic@tigetnet.mo.org
Look for us on the WebSite
PO Box 358
St. James, MO 65559
(573) 265-3899

Sullivan
"Along America's Mainstreet"

Location
Located along Interstate 44 in Crawford and Franklin Counties.

History
Originally the town was founded as Mt. Helicon in 1856. However, when the rails of the St. Louis-San Francisco Railway came through, the town's name was changed to honor one Stephen Sullivan, the donator of the land for the railroad. Stephen Sullivan had immigrated from Kentucky in 1800, and through industrious effort had amassed a considerable fortune through tobacco, as well as lead and copper mines.

➡ Getting Started

You can start your tour of this area by visiting the Sullivan Area Chamber of Commerce located at #2 Springfield.

Attractions

Fisher Cave
Tour a cave by hand-held lantern.

Meramec State Park
(573) 468-6072
Highway 185
Lots of outdoor fun along the Meramec River. Float trips are very popular.

Satellite Attractions

Purina Farms
This is primarily set up for the younger animal lovers.

✤ Leasburg
Located southwest along Interstate 44.

Onondaga Cave
(573) 245-6576
Interstate 44
Tour this popular onyx laden cave.

✤ Potosi
As far back as 1773 lead mining gave birth to this town, which was officially platted in 1826. Today it is located southeast along State Road 185.

Washington State Park
(573) 586-0322
Highway 21
Discover the ancient petraglyphs of pre-historic Indians.

❦ Stanton

This small community, named in 1850 for a powder mill operator named Peter Stanton. It is located just northeast along Interstate 44.

Antique Toy Museum
(573) 927-5555
Come see over 2,000 antique toys.

Jesse James Museum
This is located next to Antique Toy Museum.

Meramec Caverns
(573) 468-3166
Cavern tours, canoeing, and riverboat rides make this a popular attraction.

Annual Events
April
• Spring Thing
June
• Meramec Community Fair

July
• Freedom Festival
September
• Marching Band Festival
October
• Fall Festival

Shopping

Shops and restaurants are within the general area of most attractions.

In Conclusion

For more information contact:
Sullivan Area Chamber
of Commerce
PO Box 536
Sullivan, MO 63080
(573) 468-3314
FAX 573-860-2313
E-mail: chamber@fidnet.com

66 Sullivan is nestled in the foothills of the Ozarks where nature's scenery and recreational opportunities prevail. Interstate 44, known as "America's Mainstreet," connects us with both east and west, from the culture of St. Louis to the music of Branson. Sullivan is proud to offer some of the state's finest outdoor activities, wineries, and historical sites for the daytrip worth driving for. 99

—Sandi Strother, Executive Director
Sullivan Chamber of Commerce

Daytrip Missouri
Interstate 55

Cape Girardeau
"Escape to the Cape"

Location
Located in Cape Girardeau County along Interstate 55, south of St. Louis.

History
The history of Cape Girardeau is intertwined with French and Spanish roots. In 1733, a French soldier named Jean B. Girardot began a trading post that became "Cape Girardot." In 1793, under a commission by the Spanish Governor General, the frontiersman Louis Lorimier established a military post at the Cape to monitor and trade with the neighboring Indians. For a while the pioneering settlement became known as Lorimont. Later it took on its present name of Cape Girardeau.

The region became part of the United States in the Louisiana Purchase of 1803. The steamboat's ascension to prominence in 1835 made Cape Girardeau a boom town, becoming the busiest port along the Mississippi from St. Louis to Memphis. During the Civil War, Union forces occupied the strategic town and constructed four forts to guard

Cape Girardeau County Park

the river. Though the railroad enhanced Cape Girardeau's ability to grow, it was river commerce that assured the town of further prosperity.

➻ Getting Started

Begin your visit at the Convention and Visitors Bureau, located at 100 Broadway From Interstate 55, exit # 99, take Highway 61 south to Broadway, turn left and proceed east to Main (only one block from the Mississippi River).

Attractions

From history and natural beauty, to genealogy and the arts, you'll find more than you can imagine in this area.

Cape River Heritage Museum
(573) 334-0405
538 Independence Road
Housed in a turn-of-the-century fire station, this museum contains an assortment of historical and local items. Displays include exhibits on fire, police and river memorabilia; special displays include Rush Limbaugh memorabilia and the Missouri State Flag, designed and created in Cape Girardeau.

Common Pleas Courthouse
This building has been standing since 1854 During the Civil War,

it was home to Confederate prisoners. The grounds and gardens are a popular strolling place and offer a magnificent view of historic downtown area and Mississippi River.

Fort D
Giboney and Fort Streets
Four forts were constructed during the Civil War to resist assault by land and water. Fort D is the only one to remain standing.

Glenn House
(573) 334-1177
325 South Spanish
An 1883 residence featuring artistical decor of the period. Tours available.

Old St. Vincent's Church
This Gothic-styled brick structure was built in 1853 and contains more than 100 medieval period styled plaster masks. Tours are available.

William Faulkner Collection
SMSU Campus
A display of rare books, including the William Faulkner collection can be found at Kent Library.

Special Tours

The Great Murals Tour
A popular attraction in Cape Girardeau, this on-going citywide

art exhibition is displayed on various buildings around town. Self-guided sites include the Southeast Missourian Newspaper Building, where you can see "The Making of a Newspaper" depicted in underglazed ceramic stain murals. At the Kent Library there is the "Jake Wells Mural," which took nearly three years to complete. The downtown area boasts the "Jim Parker", "Riverfest ", "Riverfront Park", "Bicentennial", "Silver Coronet Band", and Missouri Wall of Fame", murals.

Rush Limbaugh Hometown Tour

The popular radio talkshow host was born and raised in Cape Girardeau. Today you can retrace the steps of the young Limbaugh as he pursued his path to success. Brochures for the self-guided tour can be picked up at the CVB office.

Mississippi River Valley Scenic Drive

Held annually in late April, this 131-mile self-driving tour offers breathtaking views of the rolling River Heritage Region. Visit quaint towns such as Altenburg, Frohna, Wittenburg, Patton, Marble Hill and join in the celebration of the heritage.

Satellite Attractions

There are an abundance of outlying attractions that merit exploration surrounding the Cape area.

Trail of Tears State Park
(573) 334-1711
Interstate 55 and Highway 57
Located 10 miles north of the city, this State Park commemorates the sorrowful march of the more than 13,000 Cherokee Indians from the Allegheny Mountains to Oklahoma, the park is home to various outdoor activities and an Interpretive Center.

Bollinger Mill State Historic Site
(573) 243-4591
Built in 1858, one of Missouri's oldest covered bridges and grist mill is located 15 miles west of Cape Girardeau Guided tours of the mill are available.

Massey House
(573) 238-3853
Marble Hill
In Bollinger County you can visit the 1869 home of Henry Massey. The oak logged structure has been completely restored and furnished to its original decor. Special tours can be arranged by calling the Bollinger County Historical Society
✪ FREE ADMISSIONS

Rocky Holler
(573) 243-6440
This recreational facility is only 5 miles north of Cape Girardeau. There you can visit a blacksmith shop, pan for gold, ride a pony, or just do some serious fishing.

Black Forest Villages
(800) 777-0068
North of the Cape on Route W
Started by Burton Gerhardt in the 1950s, this unique village contains 1870 style structures, covered bridges, and a host of crafts people who demonstrate their talents. Open to the public only during special events. Reservations required four weeks in advance.

River Ridge Winery
(573) 264-3712
Highway N
Another one of Missouri's fine wineries, this facility offers samples and snacks in the 100 year old farmhouse near Commerce, Missouri.

❧ Jackson
Named for Andrew Jackson, the county seat for Cape Girardeau County is located north along Highway 61.

St. Louis Iron Mountain and Southern Railway
(800) 455-RAIL
In Jackson you can take a ride on

an old-fashioned steam passenger train and be robbed by Jesse James or the infamous Barrow Gang. Tours include daytime and dinner trip murder mysteries.

Old McKendree Chapel
(573) 243-2774
State Road 306
This 1819 structure is reportedly the oldest Protestant Chapel standing west of the Mississippi.

Trisha's Bed & Breakfast
203 Bellevue
1-800-0408 or (573) 243-74727
Innkeepers Gus and Trisha welcome you to their 1905 Victorian home in Jackson, Cape Girardeau's county seat. Step back in time as the Wischmann's share their family history and home. Chuckle as you discover vintage lingerie collections in the 4 lovely guestrooms. Four bedrooms are available, all with private baths. Breakfast is a gourmet delight as guest feast on home-baked goodies, fresh fruits and delicious entrees

Oliver House
(573) 243-5084 .
224 East Adams Street
Another attraction in Jackson is the 1881 restored home of Robert and Marie Oliver. It was a rest stop for various historical figures. Robert's career in law and politics

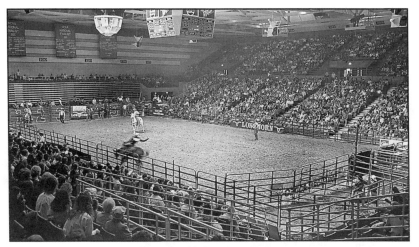

Championship Longhorn Rodeo

enabled him to entertain the likes of William Jennings Bryant, and Missouri Governor, David R. Francis. Mrs. Oliver's claim to fame was participating in the design for the Missouri state flag, that was accepted on March 22, 1913.

Harvest Weekend
A popular annual event in Jackson that occurs the first week in October, when you can enjoy pioneer crafts, old fashioned baking contest and music, along with a host of games and activities for the children.
Call (573) 243-2292 for details.

❧ Perryville
The county seat for Perry County was platted in 1822, and located just up the road along I-55. You can receive additional information to the flowing and

other worthwhile sites at the Perryville Chamber of Commerce (573) 547-6062.

Perry County Museum
Located in the Doerr-Brown House, this vintage home was built in 1881.

Faherty House
The oldest standing structure in Perryville. The house of brick and stone contains relics and furnishings of the first half of the nineteenth century.

Shelby-Nicholson-Schindler House
Another of the restored homes in Perryville.

Appleton Mill Site and Bridge and Tower Rock Natural Area
A natural attraction in the Perryville area.

Annual Events

February
• Championship Longhorn Rodeo
March
• Spring Arts and Crafts Fair
April
• Mississippi River Valley Scenic Drive
June
• Riverfest
July
• Arts and Balloon Fest
November
• Arts and Crafts Extravaganza
December
• Holiday of Lights Tour

Shopping and Dining

Just about everywhere you go you'll find shopping and dining opportunities in abundance. However, for the remote attractions, you may want to eat where the variety is greater before traveling.

In Conclusion

For further information contact:
Cape Girardeau Convention and Visitors Bureau
PO BOX 617
Cape Girardeau, MO 63702
(800) 777-0068
E-mail: Visitor @ldd.net
Web Site:
    http:\\www.capegirardeau.cvb.org

Tips

✔ There's a very scenic overlook you won't want to miss at Cape Rock.

✔ Many of the attractions at the Cape are free, however, those that charge are economically priced and certainly worth the cost.

✔ Parking may be free and plentiful, but you'll probably spend a lot of time in your car getting to the next site.

✔ Spring and Fall are well attended by bus groups, so keep this in mind if you are a single car traveler. However, parking will always be readily available in the Cape area.

✔ The Murals are a big draw to the area. It's certainly a wise idea to map the route prior to exploration.

✔ The busiest months are May and October when motor coach groups come to town.

Cape Girardeau

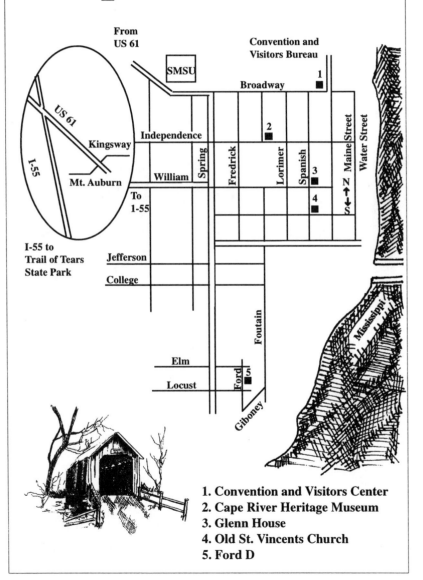

From
US 61

Convention and
Visitors Bureau

SMSU

Broadway

1

Convention and
Visitors Bureau

US 61

Kingsway

Independence

2

Mt. Auburn

William

To
1-55

I-55

I-55 to
Trail of Tears
State Park

Jefferson

College

Spring

Fredrick

Lorimer

Spanish

Maine Street

Water Street

N

S

3

4

Foutain

Elm

Ford

5

Locust

Giboney

Mississippi

1. Convention and Visitors Center
2. Cape River Heritage Museum
3. Glenn House
4. Old St. Vincents Church
5. Ford D

❝Greetings from Cape Girardeau, Missouri, Beautiful City of Roses on the River! Cape Girardeau is small town America. We have all the modern conveniences of those big cities without the side effects. We're the Big City without the "Big."

Rich with history, Cape Girardeau has been the home of many distinctive cultures such as French, Spanish, English, and German. Much of their influence is evident in the traditions and architecture.

While carefully preserving its past, Cape provides the traveler with all the modern conveniences of home such as comfortable hotel rooms and an abundance of restaurants with a variety of cuisine. From the ultra modern shopping mall to the quaint specialty shops of the historic downtown district, you're sure to find that special something here in the Cape.

No matter what season of the year you escape to Cape, the scenery surrounding the area promises a picture postcard view. You're welcome anytime! ❞

—Mary Stucker
Bureau Coordinator
Cape Girardeau Convention and Visitors Bureau

"Kennett"
"Where the Bootheel Begins"

Location
Located in southeastern Missouri along Highway 412 in Dunklin County.

History
In 1821, when Missouri attained statehood and the land was in the process of being surveyed, local landowners in the Bootheel region sought to join with the Show Me state instead of awaiting Arkansas' inevitable future entry.

Named for the former St. Louisian lawyer, Luther M. Kennett, the Bootheel town of Kennett was incorporated in 1873. With several nearby railroads passing through the area, Kennett quickly became a focal point of trade between Missouri and Arkansas. The increase of rail activity brought about an increase in the population, and Kennett soon became the population center for Dunklin County.

➡ Getting Started
True to its heritage, Kennett remains covered with a myriad of railroad tracks. Hwy 412 will take you in through the center of town. The Kennett Chamber of Commerce building is located at 1601 First Street.

Attractions

Dunklin County Museum
(573) 888-6620
122 College Avenue
Historical memorabilia, and even a 200 pound alligator gar are on display in this former City Hall. There is also a nationally recognized collection of miniature machines created by Cecil E. Anthony.

Annual Events
February
• Sons of the Western Bootheel—Friends Music
March
• River City Ramblers Dixieland Band—Friends of Music
May
• Kennett Kiwanis Rodeo
June
• Show-Me State Championship Barbecue Cookoff
September
• Delta Fair

Shopping and Dining

You'll find shopping and dining opportunities abound in the Kennett area.

In Conclusion

For further information contact:
Kennett Chamber of Commerce
1601 First Street
Kennett, MO 63857
(573) 888-5828

New Madrid
"It's Our Fault"

Location

Located along Highway 55 south of Cape Girardeau in New Madrid County.

History

The original founding of New Madrid took place in 1783 by Francois and Joseph Le Sieur. The Canadian trappers were in the employ of Gabriel Cerre in St. Louis. In 1789 the Spanish, prompted by military concerns, built El Camino Real — or the King's Highway — from St. Louis to New Madrid. In time the settlement became a popular place for the rendezvous activities of trappers. Following the Revolutionary War, an American veteran, Colonel George Morgan, received 15 million acres of land to establish a buffer colony between Spanish lands and the newly formed United States. Selecting New Madrid as his capital, Morgan began enticing settlers to move into the riverside community.

The worst of natural disasters struck the community on December 16, 1811, when settlers awoke to a massive earthquake. The event swept away islands on the river, prompted landslides that took out trees and buildings, and created huge fissures in the landscape. Even with the massive destruction of the earthquake's force, those who escaped with their lives were determined to remain, and their resolve insured the town's survival.

The constant shifting of the Mississippi's channel has on several occasions forced the moving of the town of New Madrid. In 1862, the city was attacked by General Albert A. Pope, who found it guarded by several Confederate gunboats. Pope eventually took the city through the use of heavy artillery.

Today, the small village survives as a testimony to perseverance and determination.

⇥ Getting Started

From Interstate 55, take Highway 61 to Mott Street. The Chamber of Commerce is located at 560 Mott Street.

Attractions

Hunter-Dawson Home State Historic Site
(573) 748-5340
312 Dawson Road (Route U)
See the marks of three floods on

this house originally constructed in 1858 by William W. Hunter. Large collection of original furniture.

Mississippi River Observation Deck

For a close-up view of the famous river, try this 120-ft platform on the 20-mile long "Bessie Bend" of the Mississippi River.

Mississippian Indian Mound

Adjacent to the South Interchange, (Exit #44) of Highway 61 and Interstate 55. A thousand year old mound where Hernando DeSoto is thought to have held religious services in 1540.

New Madrid Historical Museum

(573) 748-5944
1 Main Street
You can learn about everything from earthquakes to the Civil War at this facility. Also visit the Higgerson School Historic site owned by the museum.

Annual Events

June *(First Saturday)*
• Heritage Crafts Festival — The festival features traditional

working crafts of the 19th century.

July 4
• Riverfront Festival — Enjoy fireworks and have fun on the banks of the Mississippi River.

September *(3rd weekend)*
• Riverboat Days — Paddlewheeler cruises take you out on the Mississippi.

December *(2nd Saturday)*
• Christmas Candlelight tours — Experience Victorian traditions at the Hunter-Dawson Home.

Shopping and Dining

You'll find a shopper's delight in the various antique and specialty shops throughout the community. There is also a variety of restaurants.

In Conclusion

For more information contact:
New Madrid Chamber of Commerce, PO Box 96
New Madrid, MO 63869
(573) 748-5300

Tips

✔ Riverside Park for a scenic picnic

66 New Madrid, Missouri is waiting for you! We are located just three minutes off Interstate 55 via two exits #44 and #49. The oldest American City west of the Mississippi River has something for everyone. If you are looking for a small town and atmosphere with interesting things to see and do, consider New Madrid for a stop during your trip through the River Heritage region of Southeast Missouri. 99
—*Margaret PalmerDirector*
New Madrid Chamber of Commerce

Poplar Bluff
"Nature's Mining Town"

Location
Located on Highway 60 and 67 in Butler County and 60 miles west of Interstate 55.

History
Poplar Bluff was chosen as the county seat for Butler County in 1849. The area was centrally located, but at that time contained no settlement. Settlers were ferried over the Black River to the new site in rafts made with poplar logs bound together with grapevines. By 1861 when the Civil War broke out, Poplar Bluff had all of ten families and a dozen buildings.

The introduction of the Iron Mountain Railroad in 1870 assured the town of some success. With a heavy population of miners and loggers, the town took on a wild and rugged reputation.

That reputation has long since disappeared as civic pride and hard work ethics have produced a community that today prides itself as a center for trade, medicine, and education.

➼ Getting Started
You'll find the Poplar Bluff Chamber of Commerce building at 1111 West Pine Street.

Attractions

Margaret Harwell Art Museum
(573) 686-6531
421 North Main Street
View an assortment of traditional and contemporary art exhibitions here.

Moark Railroad Museum
(573) 785-4539

Old Frisco Depot
The history of railroad traveling is depicted through relics and photographs.

Poplar Bluff Museum
(573) 785-2220
1010 North Main
Butler County Historical Society showcases its memories.
✪ FREE ADMISSION

Natural Attractions

Lake Wappapello State Park
(573) 297-3232
Highway 172

Within the park is an 8,400 acre lake offering various forms of recreation.

Satellite Attractions

✻ Doniphan

Named in 1847 for Colonel Alexander Doniphan, who fought in the Mexican American War, this town is located along Highway 160 to State Road 142.

Current River Heritage Museum
(573) 996-2212
191 Washington Street
Learn about early life along the Current River. There are walking and driving tours available.

✻ Ellsinore

Located west along Highway 60.

Ellsinore Pioneer Museum
(573) 322-5404
Highway V and Cleveland Street
This has Pioneer exhibits and demonstrations can be seen.

✻ VanBuren

In 1859 this town located west along Highway 60 was appointed the county seat for Carter County.

Carter County Historical Society Log Cabin
(573) 323-4708
Courthouse Square
An 1851 restored log cabin.

Hidden Log Cabin
(573) 323-4563
John and Ash
This 1872 log cabin is furnished with period furniture.

Annual Events
January
• AG Expo
March
• Poplar Bluff Country Music Show
April
• Merchants Showcase
• Old Greenville Black Powder Rendezvous
July
• Black River Festival — The headline event in Butler County.
September
• Poplar Bluff Rodeo

Shopping and Dining
Poplar Bluff is home to a variety of shops, stores, and home-style restaurants.

In Conclusion
For more information contact:
Poplar Bluff Chamber of Commerce
PO Box 3986
Poplar Bluff, MO 63901
(573) 785-7761

66 Poplar Bluff was awarded the honor of being named the "All-American City" in 1976. A diversity of manufacturing industries has contributed to the economic growth of our city in the past 20 years. A new Community Center is utilized for numerous cultural events.

U.S. Highways 60 and 67 meet in the heart of Poplar Bluff, which is located at the southeastern edge of the Mark Twain National Forest. The forest is home to many of nature's beauties such as Big Springs National Park, Lake Wappapello, which is just minutes from Poplar Bluff and several convenient rivers and lakes that are a canoeist and tubers paradise. 99

—Ed Dust
Executive Vice President
Poplar Bluff Area Chamber of Commerce

Sikeston and Miner
"So Much More Than You Imagine"

Location
Located at the junction of I-55 and I-57/Highway 60 in Scott and New Madrid counties.

History
The history of the Sikeston/Miner area is as rich as its soil. In fact, one of the most fascinating aspects of the heritage of Sikeston/Miner is the story of the land upon which they stand. As noted on the Community Monument in the historic district of downtown Sikeston, "To know the story of this Missouri, look about you. Here from swamp and wilderness, stumps and clay our forefathers cut a home land."

—William Henry Hatch

When the first settlers came to the Sikeston/Miner region, they were welcomed by a wild and varied landscape. For it was here that oceans and rivers once ran free, cypress swamps, marshes and bayous covered the ground, bottomland forests of oak, hickory, gum, cottonwood and sycamore grew wild, and prairies stretched as far as the eye could see. The Sikeston/Miner area known as "Big Prairie", was described as "a delightful spot interspersed with beautiful groves resembling small islands in a lake."

At the beginning of the 20th century, the Little River Drainage District was formed to reclaim the land. An engineering feat, it is the largest drainage district in the nation. Today, seemingly endless fields of cotton, corn, wheat, soybeans and vegetables proclaim the richness of the legacy left by the rivers and swampland and welcome visitors to the Sikeston/ Miner area. It is here in Sikeston, founded in 1860, by a determined John Sikes who stated "I am going to start me a town and I am going to call it the town of Sikeston," and Miner, founded as a railroad town in 1902, that the Mississippi River Delta Country, begins, stretching south to New Orleans, helping to feed the world.

—Photo Jiggs Moore

Lambert's Cafe

➡ Getting Started

Start your visit with a trip to the Sikeston/Miner Convention & Visitors Bureau, located at #1 Industrial Drive. From Interstate 55, take Exit #67, travel west on Highway 62/Malone Avenue to the intersection of Malone and Selma, where you will make two immediate righthand turns. The CVB is located directly in front of the Airport in the Chamber of Commerce Building.

Attractions

So much more than you can imagine! That's what you will find when you visit Sikeston and Miner, Missouri.

Lambert's Cafe
(573) 471-4261
2515 East Malone
A visit to the legendary Lambert's Cafe, "Home of Throwed Rolls" is a must! Here, there down-home entrees are good, hot and served in an oh, so interesting fashion! You have to see it to believe it!.

River Birch Antique Gallery
(573) 472-4700
901 South Kingshighway
Antique lovers beware! Quality dealers display their fine antiques and collectibles in this new, beautifully decorated, 65,000 square foot antique gallery.

Southeast Missouri Agricultural Museum
(573) 471-3945
County Road 532, Bertrand
Boasting the largest collection of antique farm machinery in Missouri, this museum includes over 6,000 pieces of antique farm equipment — all capable of performing its original task— including some you won't find anywhere else. Also, located on the museum grounds, you will find two reconstructed Missouri log cabins (circa 1880), one wooden railroad caboose, one relocated railroad depot and a reconstructed 1920's service station.

Sikeston Factory Outlet Store
1-800-908-SHOP
100 Outlet Drive
Nearly 3 dozen factory outlet stores for your shopping enjoyment.

Satellite Attractions

From natural to historic attractions, you will find a little of everything in the Sikeston/Miner area. While you are here, consider a short trip into Missouri's Bountiful Bootheel, where you can explore large hardwood swamps, visit numerous museums interpreting the native Americans who once lived here; relive history with a trip to a civil war battlefield historic marker; drive along the banks of the Mississippi River, and see where a massive earthquake changed the face of the land in the early 1800's. For more fun, visit a winery, try your luck at a river boat casino, and let the children have fun at a hands-on-discovery museum. For more information on Missouri's Bountiful Bootheel contact the Bootheel Regional Planning Commission Tourism Committee at 1-800-976-7526 or by
E-mail: bootrpc@sheltonbbs.com

❧ **Mississippi County**

Big Oak Tree State Park
(573) 649-3149
Highway 102, 14 miles south of East Prairie
A National Natural Landmark, you won't want to miss the opportunity to visit one last surviving virgin, bottomland forests and cypress swamps in the nation.

Robert DeLaney Conservation Lake
(573) 683-6735
Highway N, north of Charleston
Fishing is a popular activity at this facility.

Ten Mile Pond Conservation Area
& No. 7 Island Conservation Area
(573) 649-2770
Highway 102, south of East Prairie
These recreation areas, managed as wetlands by the Missouri Department of Conservation, are wintering grounds for a number of waterfowl, including ducks and geese. Bald Eagles, endangered Mississippi kites, blue herons, giant blues, wild turkeys and giant Canada geese can be seen nesting here. Not only waterfowl, but deer and the rare swamp rabbit are also plentiful, and hunting and fishing opportunities abound.

Towosahgy State Historic Site
(573) 649-3149
County Road 502 off Highway 77 southeast of East Prairie
This 65-acre historic site listed on the National Register of Historic Places, preserves the remains of a once-fortified Indian village, which was also an important ceremonial center. Indians of the Mississippian Culture inhabited the site until 1400 A.D. when they apparrently burned their temples, pushed them down the side of the temple mound, and capped their ceremonial mound with clay before leaving the region. Self-guided tours are available and an interpretative exhibit provides visitors with an explanation of the mounds importance to our American culture.

❦ New Madrid County

Donaldson Point State Forest
(573) 748 5134
Hwy AB, near New Madrid
Dense timber and natural river sloughs afford many hunting and fishing opportunities and also a chance to see such species as the Bald Eagle, Mississippi Kite and Swainson's Warbler.

Hunter-Dawson Home
State Historic Site
(573) 748-5340
312 Dawson Road, Route U in New Madrid
Visit this stately antebellum home, constructed in 1858. With many original furnishings, you will feel as if you have stepped back in time to a bygone era of yesteryear.

❦ Scott County

General Watkins State Forest
(573) 748-5134
Highway 61 N, near Benton
This area contains a variety of forest types and ecosystems. Hunting, fishing, camping, hiking and nature study are popular activities.

Lake Tywappity
(573) 748-5134
Highway RA, near Chaffee
Fishing, hiking and picnicking are favorite pastimes at this nearby facility.

River Ridge Winery
(573) 264-3712
Off Highway N on County Road

321, Commerce
Situated in a century-old farm house, nestled within the hills where Crowley's Ridge joins the Mississippi River, you will find another of Missouri's fine wineries. Browse through the showroom, taste their premium wines, picnic by the river, or relax by a warm fire.

৬ Stoddard County

Mingo National Wildlife Refuge
(573) 222-3589
Highway 51, north of Puxico
This 21,676 acre refuge preserves a remnant of the vast swampland that once covered most of the Bootheel. A Visitor's center is open year round, with hiking, canoeing, fishing and nature study available during the spring and summer months.

Duck Creek Wildlife Management Area
(573) 624-7483
Highway 51, north of Puxico
Excellent fishing and hunting opportunities are available at this Missouri Department of Conservation facility.

Holly Ridge Conservation Area
(573) 642-7483
Highway 60 and Highway E, northeast of Dexter
This 1,000 acre conservation area features two natural areas, Holly Ridge and Beech Springs. Hunting, primitive camping and hiking are available.

Otter Slough Conservation Area
(573) 624-7483
Highway ZZ, southwest of Dexter
This 4,866 acre conservation area is managed primarily for species associated with wetlands, such as migratory waterfowl, mink, otter, herons, egrets and many kinds of shore birds. Open marsh areas provide natural seeds, tubers and invertebrates, all important waterfowl foods.

Annual Events

There is always something to see and do in Sikeston/Miner. For an updated calendar of events, call the Sikeston/Miner Convention and Visitors Bureau toll-free at — 1-888-309-6591

March
• Winter's Wings—Held in even-numbered years in the nearby community of East Prairie, this event offers nature lovers the opportunity to view wintering waterfowl in their natural habitat.

April
• Dogwood/Azalea Festival — Held in nearby Charleston, Missouri this festival spotlights, the vibrant flowers and colors of spring with craft bazaars, candlelight walks, a parade and more.

May
• Summerfest — Carnival, beauty pageants, and lots of daily activities highlight this five day event.

June
- NGA Hooter's Tour Pro-Am Golf Tournament — Join the play or watch the pro's go for the bucks in this exciting tournament held at Sikeston's Bootheel Golf Club.

July
- Fishing, Fireworks & Fun — Join the celebration of our nations' independence, as the Elks host their annual Youth Fishing Derby at the Sports Complex Fishing Lake and stay to watch the sky light up with a fantastic fourth fireworks display in the park at dusk.

August
- Jaycee Bootheel Rodeo — Experience the wild west at this world class championship PRCA rodeo. As Missouri's largest rodeo, this event attracts the country's top cowboys and the best in Nashville entertainment. For more information call 1-800-455 BULL.
- Redneck Bar-b-Que Cookoff — With contests, games, fun and the best darn BBQ in the land, you're sure to have a great time.

September
- Cotton Festival of the Arts — The festival where arts and agriculture meet and you can enjoy an art show, craft displays, agricultural exhibits and live entertainment.
- Cotton Carnival — In Sikeston/Miner, "cotton is king" and we celebrate the king in royal style during this festive week. A tradition for more than 50 years, this annual event features carnival rides, beauty pageants and nightly entertainment, as well as one of the largest parades in the State.
- Living History Day — Step back in time as Big Oak Tree State Park hosts this special event where modern day artisans demonstrate skills from days gone by.

October
- Red Hot Chili Cook-Off — Don't miss this tasty, annual event held at River Birch Mall.
- Octoberfest — Diebold Orchard's annual event offers the best in fall foliage, crafts and concessions.
- DARE Haunted Hayrides — Experience true fright, take a hayride into the night.

November
- Holiday Arts and Crafts Show — Find the gift with that personal touch at this craft extravaganza.

December
- City of Lights — Bus tours through the brightly lit city offer locals and visitors alike the opportunity to see Sikeston aglow with holiday spirit.

Shopping and Dining

Shopping and dining opportunities await you at every turn. From factory outlets to cozy gift shops, you are sure to find the bargain or special gift you can't resist. In addition to the homestyle flavor of Lambert's Cafe, the restaurants of Sikeston and Miner offer Mexican, American and Oriental style cuisine.

Tips

✔ Relax with a picnic or stroll in one of the cities' parks.

✔ Lambert's is a favorite attraction, plan ahead and leave yourself plenty of time to enjoy every morsel of your "throwed" rolls.

✔ The busiest months are August and September, plan ahead for heavier traffic.

✔ Visit the Gay 90's Village and bring back memories! You can purchase the antique music of yesteryear, from the 1890's and early 1900s, including nickelodeon — band organ and "carnival music."

✔ Enjoy a game of golf at the Bootheel Golf Club or Sikeston Country Club. Be sure and book a tee time.

In Conclusion

For further information please contact:
Sikeston/Miner Convention and Visitors Bureau
PO Box 1983
#1 Industrial Drive
Sikeston, MO 63801
(573) 471-6362
FAX: (573) 471-2499
Toll Free (888) 309-6591

Sikeston Jaycee Bootheel Rodeo — Missouri's Largest Rodeo

—*Photo Jiggs Moore*

66 Hello from Sikeston and Miner, Missouri — where cotton is king, our rolls are "throwed" and you are always welcome! Long the home of southern hospitality in southeast Missouri, we invite you to visit Sikeston and Miner and experience the best of Missouri's Bountiful Bootheel.

Sikeston-Miner is the home of the original, legendary Lambert's Cafe and is a beautiful agriculturally rich community with fine dining and an abundance of retail shopping opportunities, including the Sikeston Factory Outlet Stores and River Birch Antique Gallery. In Sikeston-Miner you will find a fabulous selection of overnight accommodations and year-round activities to entertain, including the Sikeston Jaycee Bootheel Rodeo — one of the largest in the Midwest. We boast the northernmost cotton production with tours and festivals celebrating "King Cotton." With 260 acres of parks and recreation, this area offers championship golf, tennis, swimming, hunting, and fishing to all of our visitors.

Sikeston-Miner is ideally located on Interstate 55 and 57, just minutes from historic landmarks, state parks, and the scenic confluence of the mighty Mississippi and Ohio rivers. So, come on, visit Sikeston & Miner, with so much more to see, do, taste and enjoy than you ever imagined. 99

—Tammy Ditto Carlyle,
Executive Director
Sikeston-Miner Convention & Visitors Bureau

CONVENTION & VISITORS BUREAU

Ste. Genevieve
"Missouri's Most Historic Town"

Location
Located on Highway 61 South of St. Louis in St. Genevieve County.

History
Ste. Genevieve, arguably the oldest permanent settlement in the state, was initially established between 1735 - 1749. The town was named for a young French girl, who in 1749, led an expedition to relieve the starving population of Paris besieged by the Franks.

One of the first names associated with the area was a Frenchman by the name of Philippe Francois Renault, who in 1723 began a lead mining operations in the area. By the 1740's, various satellite settlements had taken hold. Records of 1759 tell of a parish organized in the area called, "Poste de Saint Joachim."

In 1762 the surrounding territory was transferred to Spain and Ste. Genevieve became an outpost for the Spanish government. Unlike the English outpost on the eastern side of the Mississippi, the Creole way of

Felix Valle House

life was not disrupted in Ste. Genevieve; consequently, this greatly facilitated the growth of immigration. By 1772, the town was larger in population than nearby St. Louis.

Flooding began to plague the community early on. One of the most severe in its history was in 1785 when the city was covered by more than 15 feet of water. Though river trafficking would assist the local economy, the old town was never able to overcome its natural handicaps, and as St. Louis grew, Ste. Genevieve declined. Only by agriculture and the influx of later German settlers helped the town to survive into the twentieth century.

➡ Getting Started

You can start your visit to Ste. Genevieve at the Great River Road Interpretive Center located at 66 South Main Street.

Attractions

Amoureux House
(573) 883-7102
St. Mary's Road
Built in 1792 by Jean Baptiste St. Gemme Beauvais, this structure features upright cedar log walls set directly in the earth in the the rare poteaux-en-terre method of construction. The house is now part of the Felix Valle State Historic Site.

Bolduc-LeMeilleur House
(573) 883-3105
Main and Market Streets
This residence was built in 1820 and today stands restored for tours.

Bolduc House Museum
(573) 883-3105
125 South Main
This 1770 French Colonial home has been completely restored.

Great River Road Interpretive Center (573) 883-7097
66 South Main
Information, displays, and a gift shop are available at this attraction.

Maison Guibord-Valle
(573) 883-7544
1 North 4th Street
Formal gardens and vertical log construction highlight this 1784 construction.

Felix Valle House
(573) 883-7102
This 1818 construction used to house a company that regulated Indian trade through the region.

Ste. Genevieve Museum
(573) 883-3461
Merchant Street
Both French and Spanish history are related in relics of the period.

Bolduc House

They even have prehistoric artifacts to view.

Satellite Attractions

Hawn State Park
Route 32
(573) 883-3606
Come see the trails in Whispering Pines and Pickle Creek Natural areas.

Annual Events

February
• King's Ball — join the 200 year old tradition to choose a king and queen.
July
• Bastille Days — Lots of special events are in the historic district.
August
• Jour de Fete — This is the area's largest craft fair.

October
• Fall Harvest Festival — Come for a weekend of balloons, crafts, music and fun.
December
Plenty of holiday fun in the following:
• Annual Country Christmas Walk
• The Historic District French Christmas

Shopping and Dining

You'll find an abundance of antique stores and places to eat in the historic district.

In Conclusion

For more information contact:
Tourist Information Center
66 S. Main Street
St. Genevieve, MO 63670
(800) 373-7007

66 Ste. Genevieve, the oldest town in Missouri, boasts a wealth of two-century old homes that makes a side trip of five miles off I-55 well worthwhile. The town has preserved the small village charm of an Old World community while providing all the comforts and convenience of modern living.

Charming bed and breakfast inns, a variety of restaurants, antique and specialty shops are located in the historic district.

The largest collection of 18th century Creole structures in the U.S., make Ste. Genevieve a unique destination for travelers interested in history and architecture. Many other 19th century churches and homes blend together to add to the charm and appeal of the central square.

Spend a day in Ste. Genevieve and sample the warm hospitality that has been around for over 250 years. 99

—Fran Ballinger
Tourism Director
Tourism Information Center

Daytrip Missouri
Interstate 29

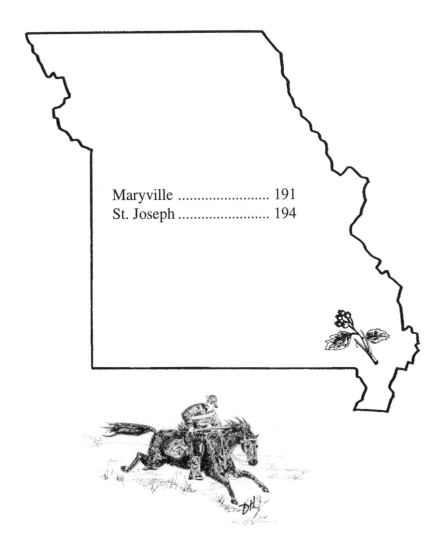

Maryville
"Heart of America's Heartland"

Location
Located in northwestern Missouri along Highway 71 in Nodaway County.

History
The region was part of the Platte Purchase in 1845. Selected as the seat for Nodaway County that year, Maryville received its name in honor of Mrs. Mary Graham, whose husband Amos was a guiding force in the new community.

Following the Civil War, an influx of freed ex-slaves and veterans from back East led to the community's growth. In 1869 when the railroad linked Maryville to Savannah, the town joined in the westward expansion of trade and profits.

In 1905 a college started as the Normal School for teachers eventually became Northwest Missouri State University.

➡ Getting Started
You'll find helpful people at the Maryville Chamber of Commerce on 423 North Market Street.

Attractions

Conception Abbey
(660) 944-2211
The Abbey is located 20 miles from Maryville. Take Route 46 to Conception Abbey on the right. Visit a Benedictine monastery founded in 1873. Abbey has been refurbished. There are retreat facilities. While visiting the Abbey, 2 miles away, at Clyde, visit the Benedictine Convent of Perpetual Adoration. Stunning mosaics and stained glass rival the churches of Europe. Beautiful grounds for a quiet, contemplative stroll.

Bilby Conservation Area
West on Route 65
Hiking, fishing, bird watching.

State Arboretum and Tree Walk
Northwest Missouri State Campus
Enjoy a tree walk on the campus.

Mozingo Lake Park
1,000 acre lake for boating, fishing

and skiing. Camping, (primitive and RV), hiking trails, picnicking, hunting and an 18 hole award-winning golf course bordering the lake.

Mary Linn Performing Arts Center
(816) 562-1212
Northwest Mo. State University
Drama and concerts are presented by professional visiting groups.

Olive Deluce Fine Arts Building
Northwest Mo. State University
Art exhibits on view.

Nodaway County Historical Society Museum
110 North Walnut
Artifacts are displayed and genealogical records are available. Visit the Historical Hickory Grove Rural School located at the museum.

Caleb Burns House
(660) 582-4955
422 West 2nd
Historical artifacts are housed in an 1844 home.

Satellite Attractions

🌿 **Albany**
Located east along Highway 136

Gentry County Historical Museum
816-726-3315

103 West Clay Street
Historical displays of Gentry County.

Special Tours
A drive through Nodaway county will enable you to see such sites as St. Oswald's in the Fields, a hundred year old Episcopal Church; the village of Elmo, where you can get a piece of homemade pie; and then Clearmont, where at the home of Lucille VanSickle, you can see weaving and antique artifacts.

Annual Events
March
- World's Smallest St. Patrick Day Parade — See for yourself if it's true.
- Home and Garden Show

June
- Citywide Garage Sale

July
- Nodaway County Fair
- Guilford Fun Day

August
- Pickering Horse Show
- Ravenwood Fall Festival
- Graham Street Fair

September
- Chamber Car Show

October
- St. Oswald's Harvest Festival — This event happens in Fairfax.

Mozingo Golf Course and Maryville Chamber of Commerce

Shopping and Dining

No need to bring your lunch here. There is lots of homestyle cooking. Motels, B&B, restaurants (fast food to fine dining).

Also, there are numerous antique, curio shops and unique shopping opportunities.

In Conclusion

For further information contact:
Maryville Chamber of Commerce
PO Box 518, 423 North Market
Maryville, MO 64468
(660) 582-8643
FAX (660) 582-3071
Web Site: maryvillemo.com

St. Joseph
"The Way to Go"

Location

Located at the intersection of Interstate 29 and Highway 36 in Buchanan County.

History

The city owes its beginnings to a visit by an employee of the American Fur Company named Joseph Robidoux. In 1799 he was sent to establish a trading post in the Blacksnake Hills. The settlement initially became known as Robidoux's Post. Located in the heart of Indian country, the site was purchased by Robidoux from the Company in 1834 for only $500.

In 1836 through the Platte Purchase by the Federal Government, an additional 2 million acres was added to the state of Missouri. Two years later when Buchanan County was organized, Robidoux's settlement became a part of it. The year 1843 saw the aging fur dealer name his town St. Joseph, after his patron saint, and in 1846, the town was established as the county seat.

St. Joseph became a rendezvous focal point for trappers during the early years, and by the 1850's, the town along the Sante Fe Trail saw its share of gold diggers. The town also became a destination point for the Hannibal - St. Joseph Railroad Company. This coupled with selection as the site of the Pony Express Headquarters in 1860 assured the area of expansive growth.

During the Civil War, Buchanan County became a battleground between Confederate guerrilla bands and Federal forces. However, following the war, St. Joseph continued to grow with the ever-increasing demands for rail shipments. The city's continued success into this century has been eclipsed only by nearby Kansas City.

➥ Getting Started

You'll want to begin at the St. Joseph Convention and Visitors Bureau. From Interstate 29 take Highway 229 west, exit to Edmond Street exit. From Edmond go down and turn left onto 4th Street. The Center will be at 109 South 4th, half a block up on the right.

Attractions

Albrecht-Kemper Museum of Art
(816) 233-7003
2818 Frederick Blvd
Works by Thomas Hart Benton, George Caleb Bingham and others are on display.

Bags End
(816) 364-1327
1023 Main
An 1866 restoration filled with St. Jo memorabilia.

Creverling's Tour House
(816) 232-9298
Built in 1880, this home features arches and massive bays.

Glore Psychiatric Museum
(816) 387-2310
3406 Frederick Avenue
More than 400 years of psychiatric history is displayed at this facility at the St. Joseph State Hospital.
❖ FREE ADMISSION

The Pony Express Monument in St. Joseph

Jesse James Home Museum
(816) 232-8206
12th and Penn Streets
The infamous Jesse was shot at this restored house on April 3, 1882.

Knea-Von Black Archives
(816) 233-6211
1901 Messanie Street
The heritage of famous national black leaders and pioneers is preserved at this exhibit.

Missouri Theater
(816) 271-4628

717 Edmond
Completely renovated 1926 movie palace which serves as a regional center for the arts.

Missouri Valley Trust
(816) 233-9192
4th and Felix Streets
An early banking establishment used by many on their trail westward.
✪ FREE ADMISSION

Mount Mora Cemetery
(816) 232-4651
824 Mt. Mora
Established in 1851, Mount Mora is St. Joseph's oldest operating cemetery and the burial site of many prominent citizens.

National Military Heritage Museum
(816) 233-4321
701 Messanie Street
Housed in the Harvey-Ellis designed building that formerly served as the city's police station. Serves as a tribute to all branches of the armed forces.

Patee House Museum
(816) 232-8206
12th and Penn Streets
Pioneer hotel and headquarters for the Pony Express in 1860. Visit the streets of ol' St. Jo, enjoy antiques, toys, art, and other attractions.

St. Joseph Museum

Pony Express Museum
(816) 279-5059
914 Penn Street
Hands-on exhibits relate the story of the glamorous Pony Express. The famous overland mail service by horseback began here on April 3, 1860.

Robidoux Row Museum
(816) 232-5861
3rd and Poulin Streets
Built in 1843 by Joseph Robidoux, this restored home contains many artifacts of the old west period of St. Jo.

Shakespeare Chateau Bed & Breakfast
(816) 232-2667
809 Hall Street
In the heart of the Hall Street Historic District is a beautiful 1885 Queen Anne mansion.
✪ Open for Tours

Schuster Mansion
(816) 233-6017
703 Hall
St. Jo's golden age is represented in this 1881 residence open for tours.

Society of Memories Doll Museum
(816) 233-1420
(816) 364-6165 for tours
12th and Penn Streets
An 1871 Baptist Church is the home of more than 600 historic dolls ranging from 1840s "covered wagon dolls" to modern variety.

St. Jo Frontier Casino Riverfront Park
(816) 279-7577
Enjoy authentic riverboat gaming at its best.

St. Joseph Fire Museum
(816) 232-1355
11th and Penn Streets
Located in Old Station #5, the fire museum houses a collection of memorabilia from the mid-1860's to present day.

St. Joseph Museum
(816) 232-8471
1100 Charles Street
Inside a Gothic mansion built in 1879, you can scan the relics of St. Jo's past. Internationally famous for its Native American displays and collections.

Tootle-Bailey Mansion
(816) 364-4072
802 Hall
Another of the Hall Street historical homes is open to tour. Built in 1890, this home features French Chauteauesque and Romanesque styles.

Twin Spires Religious History Museum
(816) 233-9788
501 South 10th Street

Jesse James Home

Stained glass windows from Innsbruck along with religious artifacts are on display here.

Arts and Entertainment

St. Joseph is home to a host of artistic and musical events. For information call (816) 364-4386. You can experience these at one of the following.
• Ice House Dinner Theatre
• Missouri Theater
• Performing Arts Association
• Robidoux Resident Theatre
• St. Joseph Symphony

Pony Express Opry
(816) 232-0955

210 North 4th Streeet
Shows 2 pm and 7:30pm, Tuesday-Saturday and 2pm Sunday.

Satellite Attractions

❧ **Maysville**
Located east along State Road 6.

Dekalb County Historical Museum
(816) 449-5542
105 North Polk
Enjoy artifacts from as far back as 1845.
✪ FREE ADMISSION

❧ Plattsburg

Located east along State Road 116.

Clinton County Historical Society Museum
(816) 930-2398
304 Birch Avenue
Tour memorabilia from the 19th century.
❂ FREE ADMISSION

Special Tours

First Street Trolley
(800) 785-0360
Convention and Visitors Bureau
Purchase an all day pass, and the trolley will take you to one or all 13 historic attractions.

Walking Tours
Information on these downtown tours can be obtained at the Convention and Visitors Bureau.

Annual Events

March
• Missouri State Championship Chili Challenge — Amateurs and professionals from the region cook up some of the tastiest chili around. Enjoy free samples.

April
• Pony Express-Jesse James Days — The Old West is recreated in this first weekend in April event.

May
• Apple Blossom Festival — Start spring with city-wide activities.

June
• Heartland Art Fest — Artists from five states combine to show their talents in everything from pottery to watercolors.

August
• Trails West! — St. Jo's largest festival, this event features re-enactments, music, food, and fun for all ages.
• St. Patrick's Fiesta — The Fiesta begins with a queen coronation dance. Festivities continue throughout the weekend with a midway and booths featuring American and authentic Mexican food.

September
• Southside Fall Festival — Bust loose at the South Side Festival and Rodeo! Three days of fun and events.

October
• Oktoberfest — Live German music, crafts, specialty booths and German-style food and beverages.
• Pumpkinfest — Pony Express Museum celebrates the spirit of fall harvest. Activities include live entertainment, arts and crafts, children's events and more.

December
• Winterfest — Holiday lights, music, and festivals.

Shopping and Dining

There is more than adequate shopping and dining facilities in St. Joseph.

Visit the Stetson Hat Factory Outlet Store, where a wide assortment of hats are available. Or tempt your taste buds at the Russell Stover Candy Outlet Store.

Then visit historic downtown and browse the many antique stores.

In Conclusion

For more information contact:
St. Joseph Convention and Visitors Bureau
PO Box 445
St. Joseph, MO 64502-0445
(800) 785-0360
(816) 233-6688
E-mail: cvb@stjomo.com
Web Site: www.stjomo.com

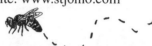

> 66 Opportunities abound to absorb St. Jo's rich history. With over 13 unique museums, numerous attractions, Victorian mansions, and fantastic celebrations and festivals, St. Jo has something to offer everyone. From the Pony Express to the Jesse James Home, you can experience the long-ago era of adventure and excitement that remains today.
>
> If you're looking for good times, take advantage of St. Jo's year-round festival season, or enjoy the arts and theater that abounds in the city. And if the outdoors is your draw, St. Jo's "greenbelt" provides a link to several of the city's parks.
>
> Whatever you're looking for, you'll find it here at Missouri's first and last frontier. 99
>
> —*Tracy Jones*
> *Communications Director*

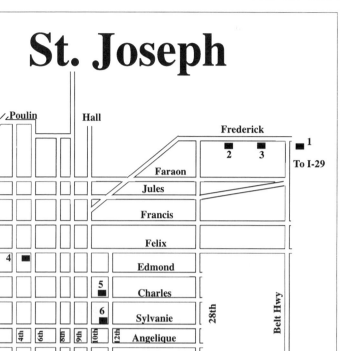

St. Joseph

1. St. Joseph Information Caboose
2. Albrecht-Kemper Museum of Art
3. Glore Psychiatric Museum
4. Missouri Valley Trust
5. St. Joseph Museum
6. Twin Spires Religious History Museum
7. St. Joseph Fire Museum
8. Knea-Von Black Archive
9. Pony Express Museum
10. Jesse James House and Patee House Museum

Daytrip Missouri
Highway 36

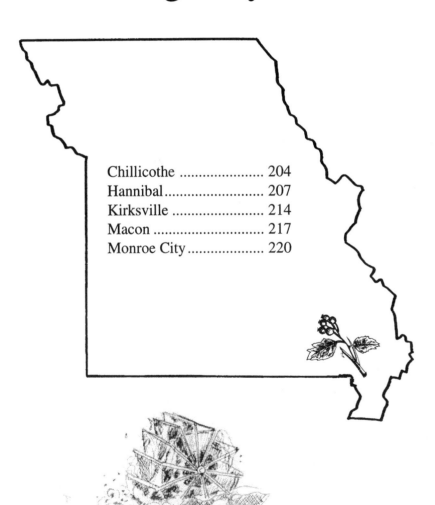

Chillicothe
"Our Big Town"

Location
At the junction of Highways 36 and 65 in Livingston County.

History
Platted in 1837 and named for its sister city in Ohio, Chillicothe became the county seat for Livingston County in 1839. Its stock went up when the Hannibal & St. Joseph Railroad brought its tracks through the town in 1859. One of the more prominent citizens from the small town was a Early Sawyer Sloan, who in the 1870's developed the world famous "Sloan's Liniment."

➥ Getting Started
You may want to stop by and visit the friendly staff at the Chillicothe Chamber of Commerce. They are located in City Hall at 715 Washington Street (Highway 65), or you may phone ahead to (660) 646-4050. Be sure to ask which of our Area Arts Council events are coming up!

Attractions

Historical Murals
Several murals depicting historical subjects have recently been commissioned. One features Graham's Mill and Covered Bridge, while another is of the once-famous Chillicothe Business College. Look for these beautiful paintings in our downtown area, which has recently undergone extensive revitalization.

Grand River Historical Society
(660) 646-4323
Located at Forrest and Irving Avenue
History dating back to the 1820's

Chillicothe Aquatic Center
Located in Simpson Park
(660) 646 6107
Open each year from Memorial Day through Labor Day. Three separate pools and water slides.

Livingston County Library
450 Locust Street
(660) 646-0547
Over 50,000 books titles and 100 magazine titles are housed in this handsome building and many services are available — Internet access, quick reference, children's services, audio visuals and the Somerville Room, a collection

Graham Mill and Covered Bridge

photo by Constitution Tribune

containing Missouri History and genealogy, as well as some information from other states.

Green Hills Golf Course
500 Mohawk
(660) 646-6669
18 championship holes, 35 bunkers; 17-acre lake; 300-yd driving range; 7,000 square feet clubhouse. Host of the 1997 Missouri Women's Golf Association Senior Championship/ PGA Pro: Russ Madsen

Satellite Attractions

❦ Jamesport — Missouri
Surrounded by the largest Amish settlement in Missouri. Open all year, except Thursday and Sunday. 16 antique shops, 4 antique malls, 26 craft/specialty shops, 4 bed and breakfasts, 8 Amish shops.

❦ Carrollton — Missouri
The current seat for Carroll County was originally settled in 1819 by John Standley, his seven sons, and John Trotter. It is located south along Highway 65.

Carroll County Historical Museum
(660) 542-1511
604 North Mason
Theme rooms depict early American life.

❧ **Laclede — Missouri**
Located east along Highway 36.

General Pershing Boyhood Home
(660) 960-2525
Highway 36 to State Road 130

Locust Creek Covered Bridge
Highway 36 to County Road Y
The longest of four surviving covered bridges in the state.

❧ **Trenton**
Named for its counterpart in New Jersey, the town, settled in 1834, is today located north along Highway 65.

Grundy County Jewett Norris Library
(660) 359-3577
Crowder and Main
An 1890 home for genealogy research.

Grundy County Museum
(660) 359-6393
1100 Mabel Street
An 1895 store houses historical exhibits.

Annual Events

July

- Freedom Festival — Independence Day Fireworks and live entertainment at Simpson Park.
- Annual Car Show — Usually the third weekend in July, this event brings many classic cars and their enthusiastic owners and fans to town. Friday night is Cruise Night and a street dance is held in conjunction with event.

September

- Chautauqua In The Park — The weekend after Labor Day each year. The main event takes place in Simpson Park with craft booths, a food court, live entertainment, storyteller's area, petting zoo, farmers' market and demonstrations. Last year brought 13,000 visitors to this event.

In Conclusion

For further information contact:
Chillicothe Chamber
of Commerce
PO Box 407
Chillicothe, MO 64601
(660) 646-4050
e:mail: cacc@greenhills.net
Web Page:
www.chillicothemo.com

Hannibal
"Home of Mark Twain"

Location

Located along Route 61 North and Highway 36 East in Marion County.

History

In 1819 Moses D. Bates platted the town we today know as Hannibal. Lumbering became a mainstay for the small village sprawled out along the banks of the Mississippi. From Hannibal's wharf, lumber and other products were shipped by steamboat to points from St. Louis to New Orleans. By 1834, log cabins gave way to more permanent brick and clapboard homes and shops.

Had a young Samuel Clemens not moved to Hannibal in 1839, no doubt the town's history would have drifted into relative mediocrity. But eventually Clemens, writing under the name of Mark Twain, brought worldwide notoriety to the town through his stories of Tom Sawyer and Huck Finn.

Mark Twain Home

Today Twain's legacy survives in Hannibal. Despite the sights and sounds of traffic lights and automobiles, echoing along the cobblestone streets in front of the boyhood Mark Twain Home. Within sight of the mighty Mississippi, you can almost hear the cries of Aunt Polly beckoning Tom to some new distasteful chore.

➥ Getting Started

You can begin at the Hannibal Convention and Visitors Bureau. Just take Route 36 to 3rd Street. On the right-hand corner you'll see the small building housing the Visitors Bureau which contains brochures, maps, and other helpful information. In addition, the State of Missouri operates the Missouri Tourist Information Center on Highway 61.

Attractions

As you stroll the cobblestone avenues around Main Street, it's easy to imagine the childhood adventures that inspired the young Clemens to later use the neighborhood as a backdrop for Tom Sawyer and friends.

Mark Twain Home and Museum Complex
(573) 221-9010
208 Hill Street
Here you'll get a sufficient edu-

cation about Twain's life to carry you through the remainder of your visit. The following are adjacent attractions:
• Mark Twain Home — An excellent restoration with period furnishings.
• Mark Twain Museum — Adjoining the Twain Home, it houses original Mark Twain editions.
• Museum Annex — Artifacts, dioramas, and a short slide presentation depict the life of Samuel Clemens.
• Clemens Law Office — The restored courtroom is where Mark Twain's father practiced law in the 1840's.
• Pilaster House/Grant's Drug Store — An 1830's construction, the Clemens family resided here in 1846-47.
• New Mark Twain Museum— Houses original Norman Rockwell paintings along with a reconstructed Pilot's House

Old Jail Museum
201 South Fourth Street
One can see restored cells in this 1878 jail as well as area fossils.

Rockcliffe Mansion
(573) 221-4140
1000 Bird
Built around the turn of the century, the exquisite home was visited by Mark Twain in 1902.

Mark Twin Riverboat

Tom and Huck Statue
Standing at the foot of Cardiff Hill, the famous piece was sculpted in 1926 by Frederick Hibbard.

The Haunted House On Hill Street Wax Museum
(573) 221-2220
Hill Street
Wax character's from Twain's books come to life at this popular attraction.

The Ice Cream Parlor
(573) 221-2336
326 North Main Street
Here you can enjoy a good ice cream and sarsaparilla while you view a display of antique toys.

Mark Twain Cave and Cave Village
(573) 221-1656
One mile south of Hannibal
This is a one-hour guided tour through a backdrop to many of Tom Sawyer's adventures.

Mississippi Riverboat Mark Twain
Center Street Landing
(573) 221-3222
Take a one-hour sightseeing or dinner cruise on this nostalgic riverboat.

**Optical Science Center
and Museum**
(573) 221-2020
214 North Main Street
5,000 square feet of optical
amusement will please the entire
family.

Sawyer's Creek Fun Park
(573) 221-8221
Highway 79 South
Enjoy shops, rides, and other
forms of family entertainment.

Entertainment

Mark Twain Outdoor Theater
(573) 221-2945
Highway 61 South
A two hour pageant portrays
many of the characters and scenes
in Mark Twain's famous novels in
this dinner-theater requiring
reservations.

**The Molly Brown Dinner
Theater**
200 North Main
(573) 221-8940
Singers, dancers, and an occasional
visit by Mark Twain himself will
entertain you at lunch or dinner.
➊ Reservations required.

Satellite Attractions

❦ Canton
The oldest town in Lewis
County was settled in 1830 and is
located north along State Road 61.

*Center for Living History
Preservation*
(573) 288-3995
Here the Civil War era comes to
life. Facilities include Wyatt Iron
Works & Visitors Center, Fort
LeSeur, and Eagle's Nest Trading
Post.
➊ FREE ADMISSION

Remember When Toy Museum
(573) 288-3995
Route B
Over 15,000 antique toys can be
seen at this facility.

❦ Kahoka
The town established in 1856
received its name from the
Gawakie Indians. It is located
north along Highway 61, and west
along Highway 136.

Clark County Historical Museum
(816) 727-3134
Morgan and Chestnut Streets
Mid-1800's displays abound.
➊ FREE ADMISSION

Special Tours

Getting around Hannibal can
be accomplished in a number of
ways. The Hannibal Trolley
Company (573) 221-1162 and the
Twainland Express Sightseeing
Tour Train (573) 221-5593 both
conduct sightseeing tours that take
you to most points of interest. It's
also quite easy to catch a quick ride
on the horse-drawn Clopper
Wagon in front of the Grant Drug

Mark Twain Cave

Store on Main Street. Prices vary but are quite reasonable.

Annual Events

May
• Mississippi River Arts Fair

July
• Tom Sawyer Days — Good food, quality crafts, and activities for the entire family.

October
• Autumn Historic Folklife Festival — Crafters and artisans bring the historic district to life in this outdoor festival featuring music, good food, and story tellers for all ages.

November
• Annual Doll Show — Hosted at the Hannibal Inn, the event features dolls, dresses, teddy bears, and crowds of collectors.
• Fiddle Championship and Music Festival — Blue Grass artists from all over.

December
• Christmas In Hannibal — Extended hours throughout the month make shopping for those 'special' gifts possible, while carolers in costume add a period flavoring to the surroundings.

Shopping and Dining

Most of the shopping is located on Main Street near the historic quarter. There you'll find an assortment of gift shops, craft and antique stores, along with a host of eating facilities.

In Conclusion

For further information contact:
Hannibal Convention and Visitors
Bureau
505 North 3rd
Hannibal, MO 63401
(573) 221-2477
Web Site: 222.han/twainweb/

TIPS

✔ Parking will probably top your agenda in reaching Hannibal. Fortunately there are several nearby locations providing free parking.

✔ There are many exhibits, shops, and eating facilities within easy walking distance from the Visitor's Bureau. Most remain open seven days a week during the summer months. Other exhibits and points of interest require a little driving to reach.

✔ Weekends are generally pretty crowded but weekdays aren't nearly as busy.

✔ After you've tired of the 'shop till you drop' syndrome, be sure to take a rest in the afternoon shade on one of the many park benches along Main Street. The thoughtful city planners of Hannibal were kind to provide a sufficient number of these for the weary tourist. A good conversation with another tired traveler usually awaits you.

> 66 Hannibal is truly America's Hometown. We who have lived here all of our lives are proud of our heritage, proud of the mid-1800's nostalgia, and proud that we can bring pleasure to world-wide visitors. Twain's small river town is our home that we share with the entire world.
>
> To make the most of your trip to Hannibal, you must visit the Mark Twain Home and Museum. Walking through these buildings will certainly make you feel as if you've entered Twain's world of the mid-1800's.
>
> Besides all of Hannibal's attractions, we have blocks of shopping in the Historical District and a variety of restaurants are scattered throughout the town.
>
> So pack up your bags and head for Hannibal, and let us share our wealth with you. 99
>
> —*Faye Bleigh, Director*
> *Hannibal Convention and Visitors Bureau*

Hannibal

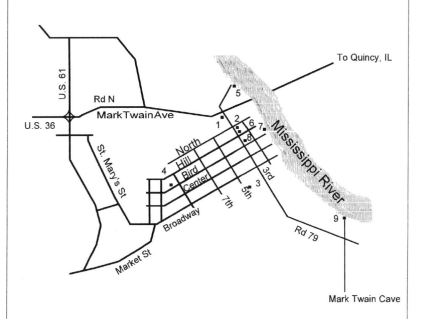

1. Visitors Center
2. Mark Twain Home and Museum
3. Old Jail Museum
4. Rockcliff Mansion
5. Tom and Huck Statue
6. Haunted House Wax Museum
7. River Boat Landing
8. Optical Science Center/Museum
9. Sawyer's Creek Fun Park

Kirksville
"In the Middle of the Heartland"

Location
Located along Highway 63 in Adair county.

History
The word 'kirk' means church; thus Kirksville literally means "village of churches." But, the town supposedly received its name from Jesse Kirk, whose wife kept the members of the original survey team well fed. The town was founded in 1841 as the seat for Adair County.

Kirksville witnessed a bloody exchange in August of 1862 when a force of 1,000 Federal soldiers under the command of Colonel John McNeil routed approximately 2,000 Confederates under the command of Lt. Colonel Joseph C. Porter near the town. This Battle of Kirksville resulted in preserving the Northern sector of Missouri under Federal control for the duration of the war.

In 1867 Joseph Baldwin established Truman University, formally Northeast Missouri State University in Kirksville. Truman is nationally recognized for its innovative assessment program and is consistently highlighted in top rankings of college guides such as Money Magazine and U.S. News and World Report.

Kirksville received additional merit in 1892 when Andrew Taylor Still began a school of osteopathic medicine. Today the College of Osteopathic Medicine enrolls more than 500 students and its reputation for excellence is nationwide.

The city was also home to the respected educator, John R. Kirk (1851-1937), whose innovations in scholastic curricula brought him acclaim throughout the state during his tenure as state superintendent of schools.

➡ Getting Started
A stop by the Kirksville Chamber of Commerce will get you the appropriate brochures and maps to get your daytrip underway. It is located at 304 South Franklin. (660) 665-3766.

Attractions

Adair County Historical Society Museum
(660) 665-6502
211 South Elson
A collection of artifacts depicting

early Adair County is contained in the museum.

🟢 FREE ADMISSION

A. T. Still Museum
(660) 626-2359
800 West Jefferson
This exhibit recounts the founding of the Andrew Still medical school.

Schwengal-Lincoln Collection
(660) 785-4537
Pickler Memorial Library, NMSU campus
Books, art and other memorabilia about Abraham Lincoln are here.

E. M. Violette Museum
(660) 785-4537
Kirk Memorial Building, on Northeast Missouri State University campus
Historical relics tell the story of life in early Northeastern Missouri.

Natural Attractions

Big Creek State Forest
One mile west of Kirksville on West Michigan Street — Plenty of outdoor fun is available on this 1,200 acre facility.

Sugar Creek State Forest
Eight miles southwest on Highway N and 11 — Over 2,600 acres are available for outdoor recreation along the creek and Chariton River.

Thousand Hills State Park
(660) 665-6995
One mile west on Highway 6 — The park surrounds the 573-acre Forest Lake. Seventeen miles of shoreline offer many opportunities for water recreation. There are cabins, camping, and a marina with a store, beach house, and restaurant at the lake. An interesting aspect of the park is the petroglyph site, an area of ancient Indian rock carvings.

Satellite Attractions

🌿 **Memphis**
Located north along Highway 36.

Downing and Boyer House Museum
(660) 465-2275
311 South Main
An 1858 mansion to tour.
🟢 FREE ADMISSION

🌿 **Novinger**
Located about 4 miles west of Kirksville along Highway 6.

Isaac Novinger Log Home
(660) 488-5280
Coal and Snyder Streets — This is a restored two-storied log cabin.

Coal Miner's Museum
(660) 488-5117
West of Main Street — The

history of coal mining is related through artifacts and exhibits

Annual Events

March
• Spring Expo
• SAA Antique Show
June
• Show Me State Games
• ElKadir Shrine Club Rodeo
July
• NEMO District Fair
October
• Red Barn Arts and Crafts Festival

Shopping and Dining

There are a number of antique and craft stores that merit exploration. Since the town is comparatively small, most of the stores are fairly close to one another. With two colleges in town, you can be assured of good places to dine.

In Conclusion

For further information contact:
Kirksville Chamber of Commerce
PO Box 251
Kirksville, MO 63501
(660) 665-3766
FAX: (660) 665-3767
Email: kvacoc@kvmo.net

Tips
✔ Much of the shopping opportunities are located along Illinois, Washington, and Jefferson streets. These run perpendicular to Highway 63.

66 Nestled in the gentle rolling hills of Northeast Missouri, Kirksville shines in the quality of life offered to it residents. This forward moving community offers numerous lakes and state parks with great hunting and fishing to challenge nature lovers of all types. Kirksville offers the best to both the body and the mind. A well-rounded, family-oriented community awaits you in Kirksville. 99

—Roseann Wheeler
Executive Director
Kirksville Chamber of Commerce

Macon
"The City of Maple"

Location
Located at the intersection of Highways 63 and 36 in Macon County.

History
The town of Macon was first settled by James T. Haley in 1852. However, long before Mr. Haley's arrival, scores of immigrants from Kentucky and Virginia ventured into the region as early as 1829. A nearby trail, called the Bee Trace, became a popular pioneers' path to search for honey. This pursuit brought many travelers through the region. Later, deposits of coal would bring vital industry to the area.

In 1856 the town was laid out and platted. In an unusual circumstance both town and county were named after Nathaniel Macon, a Revolutionary War veteran from North Carolina. Mr. Macon had served in the House of Representatives from 1791 to 1816. In 1863 the county

One of the last Drive-Ins in Missouri

seat was moved from Bloomington to Macon.

Today Macon has been called everything from "The City of Maples" to "Macon, Country Air with a City Flair." Each of these names attests to the wholesome environment preserved here.

➡ Getting Started

Though there is much history in Macon County, you'll find that the name of the game here is outdoor fun. However, you may find a visit to one of the many annual events, or a day's search for antiques more to your daytrip liking. The Macon Chamber of Commerce office is located at 300 North Rollins, Suite 102 A.

Attractions

Blees Building

This 1899 structure built by Fredrick Blees was initially used as a military Academy.

Blees Museum

(816) 385-3372
North Rollin
Macon County historical artifacts are on display.

Long Branch Lake and State Park

(816) 385-2108
West of Macon along Highway 36
This nearly 2,500 acre lake is home to a host of outdoor recreation activities and has panoramic scenery. Boat ramp, swimming beach, and marina are all on hand.

Macon County Court House

This is one of the oldest buildings in town.

Thomas Hill Wildlife Area and Lake

(816) 785-2420
Highway C
In the middle of this nearly 6,000 acre park is the 5,000 acre Thomas Hill Lake. A full slate of outdoor recreation is on tap here.

Annual Events

May
• Mother's Day Spring Tea and Doll Show — This takes place at the Blees Museum.

June
• Outlaws Rodeo
• Bee Trace Festival —This annual event at the Long Branch State Park is the headliner for the area. Crafts, costumed re-enactors, and festivities.

August
• Maple Leaf Festival

September
• New Cambria Fall Festival
• LaPlata Soy Bean Festival

October
• Loch Haven Quilt Show

November
• Loch Haven Craft Show

December
- Christmas at the Blees Museum

Shopping and Dining

The downtown offers a wide variety of stores including arts and crafts. And the Macon restaurants will satisfy any appetite.

In Conclusion

For further information contact:
Macon Area Chamber of Commerce
300 N. Rollins Suite 102 A
Macon, MO 63552
(816) 385-2811

> 66 Macon has not only stately buildings but friendly people. There are over 12 antique shops that offer a wide variety of merchandise.
>
> For the hunter, Macon County has been #1 in deer harvested for the past several years. For the fisherman, Long Branch Lake and Thomas Hill will satisfy your "fishin' fever."
>
> Looking for a place to relax? Come to the Macon Area — a growing community with friendly people and a place to watch the seasons change in all their splendor. A place to relax and breathe clean, fresh air. Come try the good life! Macon. 99
>
> *—Crystal Lyda*
> *Executive Director*
> *Macon Chamber of Commerce*

Monroe City
"Gateway to the Mark Twain Lake"

Location
Located at the juncture of Highway 36 and 24 in Monroe County.

History
This town was originally platted in 1857 by E. B. Talcott. The area had attracted a number of settlers from Kentucky and Tennessee. Monroe City was intended to be a shipping point on the Hannibal and St. Joseph Railroad. Though Southern sympathies prevailed at the outbreak of the Civil War, the city was controlled early on by Federal forces.

Today Monroe City, known as the Gateway to the Mark Twain Lake, was once considered northeastern Missouri's major provider of poultry and eggs.

➡ Getting Started
Monroe City caters to the outdoor enthusiast. However, there are also many things to do and see for an indoor daytrip. The Monroe City Chamber Office is located at 314 South Main.

Attractions

Mark Twain Lake State Park
(573) 565-3440
Highway 107
An 18,600 acre lake offers plenty of recreational facilities.

**Clarence Cannon Dam
and Power Plant**
Adjacent to Mark Twain Lake
Named for one of Missouri's outstanding U. S. Representatives, the facility offers tours.

Saint Jude's Episcopal Church
This oldest church in Monroe City was built in 1867.

Entertainment
Ozark flavored country music is provided by midwestern acts at the following:

Cannon Dam Opry
(573) 565-3287
Highway 19 and 154

Grandma's Country Music Show
(573) 672-3202
Highway 107

Salt River Opry
(573) 735-4461
Route J

Satellite Attractions

❦ Bethel

This German community, just north along State Road 15, was started in 1845 as a commune.

Bethel German Colony

(816) 284-6493
Main Street
This 1844 German community is worth a visit.

❦ Florida

Established in 1831, this small hamlet lies south along Route U.

Mark Twain Birthplace

(573) 565-3449
Highway 107 and Route U
A modern museum houses much of Mark Twain's memorabilia, including the restored two-room cabin in which he was born.

❦ Paris

One of the older towns in Monroe County, Paris was founded in 1831. It is located west along Highway 24.

Allen Home

Highway 15
Visit this 1869 residence.

Brace Home

Rock Road
An 1850 restored residence.

Broughton House

316 East Madison

This 1831 structure was the original home for the Baptist Congregation.

Robert Burgess House

316 West Monroe
An 1860 French mansard style home.

Clay Mallory Home

328 West Marion
The oldest house in the village.

Thomas Conyer House

122 Payne Street
Constructed in 1845, much of the original portion is still in use.

Monroe County Courthouse

(816) 327-4611
This majestic 1912 structure houses several murals and Historical Society Museum.

Judge D. H. Moss Home

403 West Locust
An 1884 Queen Anne style home.

Union Covered Bridge

Highway C
This 125 foot long bridge was built in 1871 by Joseph C. Elliot.

Annual Events

July
- Mark Twain Lake Rodeo
- Monroe County Fair

August
- Salt River Folk Life Festival

October
- Missouri Mule Days

December
- Tour of Lights
- Live Nativity

Recreation

**Mosswood Meadows
Golf Course**

There is a beautiful 9-hole golf course that sets at the western edge of Monroe City on Highway 36. It features watered fairways, bent grass greens, putting greens, driving range, Pro Shop and a snack bar.

Shopping and Dining

You'll find an assortment of country craft and antique stores along with a full spectrum of eating facilities in the Monroe City area.

In Conclusion

For further information contact:
Monroe City Chamber of Commerce
PO Box 22
Monroe City, MO 63456
(800) 735-4391.

---

66 Outdoor fun abounds on beautiful Mark Twain Lake. This 18,600 acre reservoir lake located just south of Monroe City opened in 1983 and provides fishing, swimming, camping, and boating pleasures. The lake's 285 miles of shoreline are filled with wildlife for hunting.

Monroe City offers many conveniences in a friendly, small town atmosphere. You'll find several home-style-restaurants, and antique shops are easily accessible.

To the south, overlooking Mark Twain Lake, is the small village of Florida with the cabin in which Samuel Clemens, known often as Mark Twain, was born.

Come to Mark Twain Lake near Monroe City for outdoor fun and small town hospitality. 99

—Dotty McGarry
Executive Secretary
Monroe City Chamber of Commerce

Maps

Interstate 70

Interstate 44

Interstate 55

Interstate 29

Highway 36

224 • PHOTO CREDITS

Photo Credits

The staff of Daytrip Missouri would like to acknowledge and thank the following contributors of photos for the second edition of the daytrip book.

- Auto World Museum and Kingdom Expo Center
- Boonville Chamber of Commerce
- Branson/Lakes Area Chamber of Commerce and Convention and Visitors Bureau
- Cape Girardeau Convention and Visitors Bureau
- Carthage Chamber of Commerce
- Chillicothe Chamber of Commerce
- Columbia Convention and Visitors Bureau
- Convention and Visitors Bureau of Greater Kansas City
- Friends of Arrow Rock
- Ha Ha Tonka State Park
- Hannibal Convention and Visitors Bureau
- Hermann Visitors Center
- Independence Tourism Department
- Jefferson City Convention and Visitors Bureau
- Joplin Convention and Visitors Bureau
- Kingdom of Callaway Chamber of Commerce
- Lake of the Ozark Convention and Visitors Bureau
- Macon Area Chamber of Commerce
- Maryville Chamber of Commerce
- Mexico Chamber of Commerce
- Moberly Chamber of Commerce
- Missouri Division of Tourism
- Nevada/Vernon County Chamber of Commerce
- Precious Moments Chapel
- Rolla Chamber of Commerce and Tourist Center
- Sedalia Area Chamber of Commerce
- Sikeston/Miner Convention and Visitors Bureau
- Springfield Visitor and Convention Center
- Ste. Genevieve Tourist Information Center
- St. Joseph Convention and Visitors Bureau
- St. Louis Convention and Visitors Bureau
- Tourism Information Center Ste. Genevieve
- Westminster College
- William Woods University

Travel Log Memories

Location:

Date:

Place Visited:

Those Present:

Best Memories:

Travel Log Memories

Location:

Date:

Place Visited:

Those Present:

Best Memories:

Travel Log Memories

Location:

Date:

Place Visited:

Those Present:

Best Memories:

Travel Log Memories

Location:

Date:

Place Visited:

Those Present:

Best Memories:

Travel Log Memories

Location:

Date:

Place Visited:

Those Present:

Best Memories:

Travel Log Memories

Location:

Date:

Place Visited:

Those Present:

Best Memories:

Index

Symbols

—*from Kansas City Visitors Center*